LARRY D. BARNETT

THE BIOSPHERE AND HUMAN SOCIETY

Understanding Systems, Law, and
Population Growth

BRISTOL
UNIVERSITY
PRESS

First published in Great Britain in 2023 by

Bristol University Press
University of Bristol
1–9 Old Park Hill
Bristol
BS2 8BB
UK
t: +44 (0)117 374 6645
e: bup-info@bristol.ac.uk

Details of international sales and distribution partners are available at
bristoluniversitypress.co.uk

© Bristol University Press 2023

British Library Cataloguing in Publication Data
A catalogue record for this book is available from the British Library

ISBN 978-1-5292-3248-6 hardcover
ISBN 978-1-5292-3249-3 ePub
ISBN 978-1-5292-3250-9 ePdf

The right of Larry D. Barnett to be identified as author of this work has been
asserted by him in accordance with the Copyright, Designs and Patents Act 1988.

Cover design: blu inc.
Front cover image: Stocksy/Kike Arnaiz
Bristol University Press use environmentally responsible
print partners.
Printed and bound in Great Britain by CPI Group (UK) Ltd,
Croydon, CR0 4YY

FSC
www.fsc.org
MIX
Paper | Supporting
responsible forestry
FSC® C013604

To
Linda Rae, my wife and friend

Contents

List of Figures and Tables

Figures

Tables

Preface

For most scholars, human overpopulation as a subject for study requires a hard sell. That, however, was not true for me. My childhood was spent in southern California during the 1940s and 1950s, and I thus personally saw a beautiful area fall victim to growth in the number of people. This experience led me to have a long-standing interest in the field of demography and in how the numerical size of the human population affects the natural world and the social life of human beings. Unfortunately, however, the effects of human overpopulation are subtle and, therefore, generally unappreciated. *The Biosphere and Human Society* and its predecessor, *Demography in the Anthropocene* (published in 2021), summarize the evidence that the natural and social sciences have developed, especially in recent years, regarding the deleterious consequences of the number, and increases in the number, of humans. The two books complement one another, and my hope is that together they will underscore these consequences and will stimulate scholarship on humanitarian ways to end the numerical growth of *Homo sapiens*.

Let me mention, too, that *The Biosphere and Human Society* elaborates on my May 2021 blog 'Population Dynamics, the Concept of a "System," and the Law of Unintended Consequences.' The blog is at https://overpopulation-project. com/population-dynamics-concept-of-system-and-law-of-uni ntended-consequences.

I would be remiss if I closed without acknowledging the members of the library staff at the Widener University Delaware Law School, especially Christy D'Antonio. The staff responded expeditiously to requests I submitted for copies of publications that I was unable to access. The assistance was invaluable and added immeasurably to my ability to write the chapters that follow.

Larry D. Barnett
Wilmington, Delaware, August 2022

ONE

Paradigms, Environmentalism, and Demography

In one noteworthy respect, scholarship is comparable to a chain—just as a chain cannot be stronger than its weakest link, a scholarly project cannot be better than its lowest-quality component. Accordingly, whether scholarship utilizes numeric data or relies on non-numeric information, its output will suffer if any part of the scholarship is problematic. With this in mind, I turn to a key component of scholarship, viz., paradigms.

1.1 Paradigms in scholarship

Paradigms play an important role in scholarship because they involve the assumptions that direct scholars to the phenomena that should be studied and tell scholars how to study the phenomena.[1] A paradigm that is defective can, therefore, hold back scholarship and the advance of knowledge.[2] Although a discipline that uses a faulty paradigm may still add to the store of knowledge,[3] it would make greater contributions, and/or would make the contributions sooner, if its paradigm was not defective. A faulty paradigm is, then, manifestly undesirable. Of course, scholars in every discipline want to avoid a faulty paradigm, because their output must eventually be useful, and when disciplines differ in the utility of their scholarship, they will differ in financial support and prestige. The marketplace of ideas, in brief, gives scholars a strong incentive to be on guard against flaws in their paradigms. Nonetheless, recognizing and removing established paradigm flaws is not easy and does not occur quickly.[4]

In law, scholarship employs several paradigms and appears to be adding more,[5] probably because law draws on many non-law disciplines.[6] Naturally, not all non-law disciplines beneficial to law are static; at least some of them are in flux. As a result, paradigm evolution occurs, and indeed is required, in law and its areas of specialization. Such evolution is particularly needed in environmental-law scholarship, because the paradigm of environmental law at the present time ignores a key cause of the damage that has been and is being done to the biosphere. However, in ignoring a principal source of damage to the biosphere, environmental law is not alone. The paradigm in the field of 'sustainability science,' for example, is neglecting this cause, too, and hence is proving unable to solve problems that are relevant to it.[7] Consequently, environmental law as well as sustainability science—disciplines that are obvious allies[8]— need to amend or replace their current paradigms. Unless and until they do so, their ability to alleviate, let alone eliminate, pertinent problem-causing agents will be severely limited.

1.2 The paradigm in environmentalism

In the present book, I hope to persuade scholars who use the now-popular paradigms of environmentalism to alter those paradigms. Specifically, I point to the numerical size and growth of the human population, a phenomenon that is left out of the current focus of environmental law and other environmentally concerned disciplines.[9] This omission is as regrettable as it is important:[10] The numerical growth of the human population has been central to the onset, and will be key to the intensity, of the Anthropocene. As a result, human-population growth, by reducing '[b]iodiversity and nature's regulating contributions to people,'[11] is putting the future of *Homo sapiens* in danger.[12] Scholars in environmental disciplines may believe that the biosphere of the planet has been hurt by economic growth rather than by population growth, but the degradation of the biosphere is not solely due to economic growth. Despite disagreement over the relative importance of each factor, both of them harm the biosphere, and population growth cannot be simply brushed aside.[13] Unfortunately, however, population growth and ways to halt it are off-limits as a topic for consideration today.[14]

In confronting the phenomenon of human-population growth, we should, however, be mindful of a key point: Population growth occurs in social setting, not in a social void. I thus tie population growth to human society and to a critical property of every human society, viz., the existence and operation of a society as a *system*. Otherwise said, human fertility, mortality, and migration—the demographic processes that determine population size—are products of human societies and, hence, of systems. Law and government policy, too, arise and operate within societal systems. In short, environmentalism must incorporate population growth and the social-system context of population growth into its thinking, and until it does, environmentally oriented scholarship and the solutions it proposes to biospheric problems will suffer.

I note that, while some human societies in the past may have experienced large, rapid declines in the number of people in their populations because population size had gone beyond what was supportable by the biosphere, the evidence advanced for this possibility has been questioned.[15] Nonetheless, population overshoot and collapse cannot be summarily dismissed in light of a recent study that modeled such an event in Europe during the fourteenth century A.D.[16] Moreover, population overshoot and collapse is a distinct possibility today.[17] The prudent course of action for *Homo sapiens*, therefore, is to avoid having a population that is too large. Failure to prevent overpopulation, and reduce excessive human numbers, may have severe consequences—consequences that may develop suddenly and, at least in the short run, be irreversible. In other words, signals backed by credible evidence ought not to be ignored when they flash orange or red and tell us that the number of human beings on Earth is approaching, and may have already exceeded, the population size that can be adequately and permanently supported.

Let us look briefly at such a signal. According to the estimates in Figure 1.1,[18] amounts and types of resource consumption and disposal across the countries of the world have, since the 1970s, demanded more than one Earth to supply the human population with enough 'biologically productive land and water ... to produce all the resources it consumes and to absorb the waste it generates, using prevailing technology and resource management practices.'[19] Figure 1.1 shows, too, that this human-created pressure on the biosphere has been undergoing a secular increase over time and that the increase has been substantial. Notably, for almost the entire period since 2010, roughly 1.7 Earths were necessary to take care of the human population. In short, far too much is being asked of the planet by its human population.

Unfortunately, scientists have not definitively identified the precise threshold at which the numerical size of the human population passes the threshold that triggers severe reactions in the biosphere.[20] Furthermore, this threshold may not be constant over time, and it may be reduced by human activities that degrade the biosphere. The 'ecological footprint'[21] of *Homo sapiens* graphed in Figure 1.1 should be of deep concern, therefore, because it indicates that the population of human beings presently on the planet has exceeded, and is increasingly exceeding, what the biosphere can supply given prevailing levels and patterns of resource consumption and disposal. Notably, other evidence also leads to this conclusion.[22] In effect, *Homo sapiens* has been a borrower from a biospheric bank, and it may be a reckless borrower because it may lack the wherewithal to cover the loans that it has taken out.

Remarkably, humans appear to have just minimal awareness of the damage that the numerical size of their population is

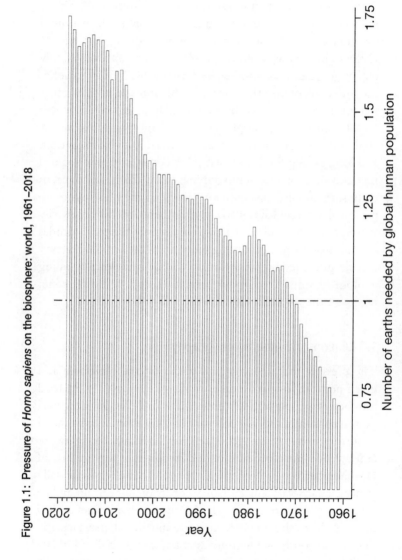

Figure 1.1: Pressure of *Homo sapiens* on the biosphere: world, 1961–2018

Source: Data from Global Footprint Network; graph by author (see note 19 in this chapter).

inflicting on the biosphere. Of course, from one perspective, the lack of widespread and intense interest in overpopulation should not be surprising. Hominids have been on Earth for millions of years,[23] and modern *Homo sapiens* has been around for millennia—by one estimate, for around 141,000 years.[24] Overpopulation as a global problem is thus an exceedingly recent development, and given social inertia, human societies do not yet recognize the role of population size in generating significant societal concerns even though these concerns cover a wide range, for example, crime and inter-group conflict, epidemics of high-fatality disease, elevated levels of migration, and long-lasting food insecurity.[25] A corollary of the societal incognizance of the demographic cause of these concerns is, unsurprisingly, that individual societal members who are personally worried about the environment are not necessarily worried about population growth. Certainly, the two attitudes are not strongly related among residents of the United States,[26] this despite the disproportionately large and long-standing ecological impact of Americans.[27] In the Anthropocene, however, the two attitudes ought to be tightly linked.

1.3 Lessons in human demography

The pressure that *Homo sapiens* places on the biosphere at a given point in time is a function of two factors—(1) the total number of people and (2) how much the average individual person consumes and, as a corollary of consumption, how much waste the average person generates. Arithmetically, the aggregate amount of human pressure on the biosphere is the product of (1) multiplied by (2). Nonetheless, present-day environmentally concerned scholars concentrate generally on just (2) and, unlike a half-century ago, ignore (1).[28] Among environmental-law scholars, the neglect of population size and growth may be partly due to the youth of environmental law as a specialty.[29] In any environmentally oriented discipline, however, the neglect of the population factor is curious, and there are at least three reasons why. The first is that many of the problems that *Homo sapiens* confronts at the present time, and appears likely to continue confronting for decades to come, are exacerbated if not created by the numerical size and/or growth of the human population.[30] The second reason is that environmentally concerned scholars are presumed to be cognizant of, and to pay attention to, all types of agents that pose a threat to the biosphere. Indeed, these scholars have been drawn to, if not accepted, the concept of the Anthropocene, and although the Anthropocene has not yet been formally recognized as a geological epoch,[31] it is, by definition, a period in which human beings are a major, if not the principal, source of global change in the biosphere.[32] The demographic dimensions of *Homo sapiens*, in short, are obviously relevant in the Anthropocene, and the lack of concern in the paradigm of environmentalism with the number of humans on the planet is puzzling.

The absence of human-population size and growth from the paradigm of environmentalism is odd for a third reason as well. Since this reason is more complicated than the first two, it requires a lengthier discussion. Globally, the numerical size of the population of *Homo sapiens* is steadily increasing even though the rate of population growth and rates of age-specific fertility have come down. The numerical expansion of the human population each year, moreover, is considerable. However, because environmentalists have failed to engage with demography, they have not grasped the difference between the course of change in numerical additions to the human population, on the one hand, and the course of change in the rate of human-population growth and in age-specific fertility rates, on the other. The absence of an understanding of the difference, in turn, appears to have led environmentalists to discount the numerical size and growth of the human population as an agent in environmental degradation. As a result, underscoring the difference—a task that I undertake next—may help to promote an appreciation of the importance of the number of human beings to the biosphere.

1.3.1 Numerical growth and rate of growth of the human population

All else being equal, the pressure on the biosphere that is created by human beings mounts as the numerical size of the population of *Homo sapiens* becomes larger, and even if the pressure per person declines, increments in population size can offset the per capita decline. Critically, while growth in the number of people occupying planet Earth occurred slowly for a long time, it has been large in absolute amount for decades.[33] Figure 1.2, which is derived from data published by the United Nations Population Division, includes two gauges of yearly change in the global human population since the mid-twentieth century.[34] One gauge is the *number* of people added to the human population of the planet from the middle of one year to the middle of the following year. These numbers, in millions, are represented by the vertical bars in the inner region of Figure 1.2; the numeric values for the bars are shown on the left vertical axis. The second gauge is the *rate* at which the population of *Homo sapiens* increased annually, that is, the percent changes in population size from the middle of one year to the middle of the next. The rates are represented by the solid line in the inner region of the figure; the numeric values for the line are shown on the right vertical axis.

Figure 1.2 tells us that the world has had a gain of no less than 79,000,000 people each year since 2000; in the latest year, which covers mid-2019 to mid-2020, the gain exceeded 81,000,000 people. Figure 1.2 also reveals that numerical growth can be substantial even though the growth rate is falling. Indeed, during a period in the early twenty-first century, numerical growth increased while the growth rate decreased. The reason for this divergence is mathematical—the size of the base to which the yearly growth rate applied was becoming larger, and the enlargement of the base more than made up for the reduction in the growth rate.[35]

Figure 1.2: Yearly numerical and rate of growth of the human population of the world since the mid-twentieth century

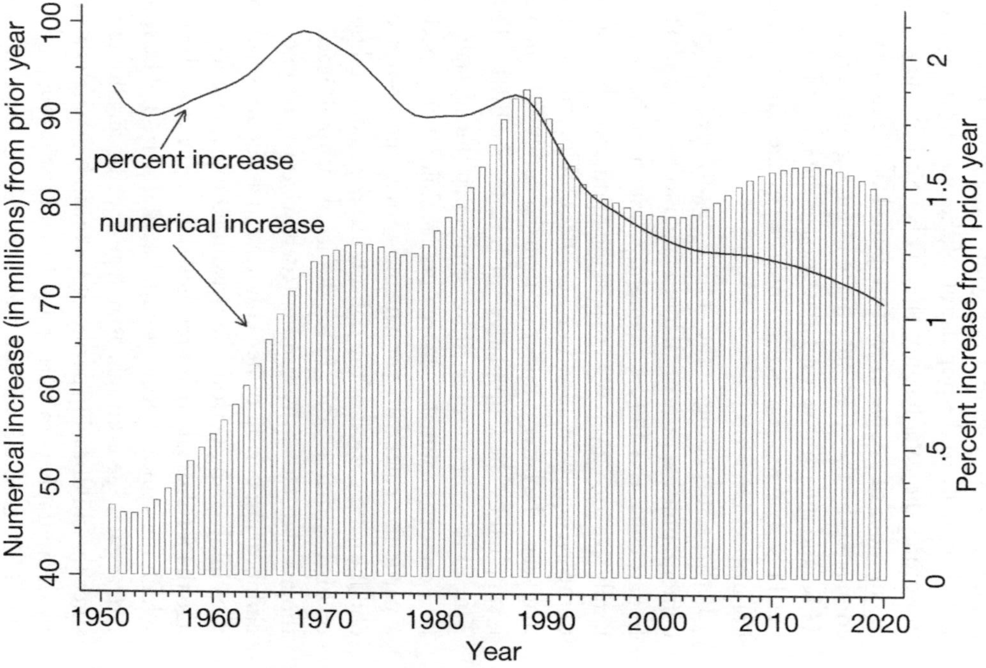

Source: Data from United Nations; calculations and graph by author (see note 34 in this chapter).

1.3.2 Numerical growth of the human population and the total fertility rate

Figure 1.3, like Figure 1.2, includes the number of people added annually to the population of the world, but Figure 1.3 substitutes the total fertility rate (TFR) for the rate at which the number of people grew. In Figure 1.3, the hollow circles connected by the solid line in the inner region represent the TFR, and the right vertical axis displays the numeric values of the TFR. Figure 1.3 uses data published by the United Nations Population Division.[36]

Perhaps surprisingly, the TFR, despite being a popular demographic measure of childbearing, is often misunderstood. In particular, the TFR is frequently thought to be completed family size for a given year, that is, the number of children born to the average woman who exited her childbearing period in that year. The latter number (completed family size), however, is supplied by the Cumulative Birth Rate, not by the TFR.[37] The TFR is the number of live births that the average female in a cohort of females that enters its childbearing period in a particular calendar year will have over the course of the childbearing period of the cohort, but the calculated number of births (that is, the TFR) comes with qualifications — the average female is assumed to survive to the end of the childbearing period of her cohort, and as she moves through the childbearing period, she is assumed to experience at each age the fertility rate that prevailed during the calendar year in which her cohort began its childbearing period. The fertility rate at each age is known as an 'age-specific fertility rate,' and since the childbearing period of a woman is generally assumed by demographers to start at age 15 and last through age 49,[38] the TFR is based on—or, more exactly, is the sum of—35 age-specific fertility rates. The TFR is thus a projection of 'the mean number of children who would be born to a woman during her lifetime, *if* she were to spend her childbearing years conforming to the age-specific fertility rates that have been measured in a given year'[39] and lives until her 50th birthday, the age when and after which the incidence of childbearing is presumed to be zero. As the TFR considers the age-specific fertility rates in a particular year to remain constant over time, the TFR is a measure not of actual fertility but, rather, of the fertility that would occur under an unchanging set of age-specific fertility rates, viz., the rates that obtained in the year for which the TFR is calculated. Of course, age-specific fertility rates vary from one year to another, and hence the TFR will differ between years.

An understanding of what the TFR measures (and does not measure) may be facilitated by an illustration of how the TFR is calculated. To show the calculation procedure, I use data for the world as a whole during the time interval 2010–2015. The first column of the three columns in Table 1.1 lists five-year age ranges (rather than single years of age) in which females are assumed to be capable of bearing children. For each of the five-year age ranges, the second column presents estimates, published by the United Nations Population Division, of the mean fertility rate in the world as a whole.[40] The third column, which is based on the second column, reports the aggregate fertility rates within each age range. Because every age range in the example includes five years (seen in column 1), the rates in the second column were multiplied by five to obtain the rates in the third column. The third column thus supplies global age-specific fertility rates in 2010–2015 for all females in the five-year age ranges of the childbearing period, that is, shows the number of births per 1,000 childbearing-capable females during 2010–2015. As the third column reveals, the TFR, expressed as the projected mean number of lifetime live births to females whose fifteenth birthday occurred during 2010–2015, was 2,517 live births per 1,000 women, or 2.517 live births per woman.

The preceding discussion may help the reader to interpret the TFR and Figure 1.3. The TFR is shown in Figure 1.3 for the midpoints of successive five-year intervals, with the first

Table 1.1: Total fertility rate (illustrative calculation)

Age range	Number of births per 1,000 females (mean of age range)	Number of births per 1,000 females (all ages in age range)
15–19	46.7	233.5
20–24	142.9	714.5
25–29	142.0	710.0
30–34	99.7	498.5
35–39	51.4	257.0
40–44	16.8	84.0
45–49	<u>3.9</u>	<u>19.5</u>
	$\Sigma = 503.4$	$\Sigma = 2517.04$

TFR being at the midpoint of 1950–1955, the second TFR being at the midpoint of 1955–1960, and the last TFR being at the midpoint of 2015–2020. As the figure reveals, the TFR of the world population is much lower today than it was in the middle of the twentieth century: In the early 1950s, live births per woman were projected to be roughly five, but just seven decades later, a woman was projected to produce only half this number of children. Nonetheless, the long-term downward trend in the TFR from the midpoint of the last century to the present time has not prevented yearly growth of the world population from being large and becoming larger.[41] For example, during the 1950s, world population grew by less than 54,000,000 people annually; from 2005 onward, growth has exceeded 80,000,000 people annually.

To understand the substantial growth of the global population, a further aspect of the TFR must be kept in mind: A particular numeric value of the TFR does not by itself reveal whether a population is at, above, or below 'replacement-level fertility,' that is, the mean number of live births per woman that eventually produces a stable population size.[42] The exact mean number of live births per woman at which a population will stop growing can differ across populations and across time,

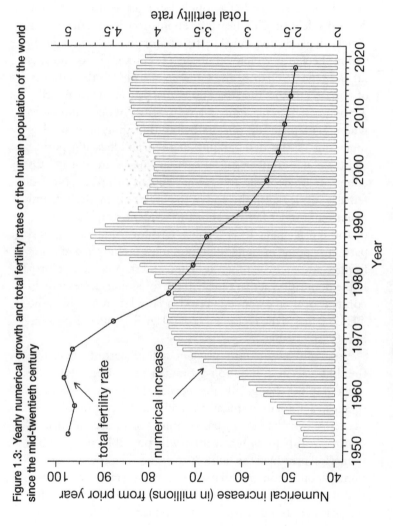

Figure 1.3: Yearly numerical growth and total fertility rates of the human population of the world since the mid-twentieth century

Source: Data from United Nations; calculations and graph by author (see notes 34 and 36 in this chapter).

that is, can differ between two or more populations at a single point in time and can also differ within a single population between two or more points in time. Such differences are possible because whether a population replaces itself does not depend solely on childbearing. Population replacement in a society depends, too, on (1) rates of mortality among females before the age at which childbearing is presumed to end and (2) the ratio at birth of the number of males to the number of females, that is, the sex ratio.[43] A mean of two live births per woman is replacement-level fertility when, and only when, (1) females do not die before the aging process takes them out of the demography-defined childbearing period *and* (2) equal numbers of females and males are born.[44] Of course, neither of the foregoing happens in reality: Not all females survive until the end of the childbearing period, and males outnumber females at birth.[45] A demographic estimate of the replacement-level fertility rate for a population at a particular point in time, therefore, must employ age-specific fertility rates, female mortality rates, and the sex ratio at birth in the population at that time.[46] If the foregoing factors remain constant over an extended period, a population in which the TFR is equal to the replacement-level fertility rate will become numerically stable.[47]

Essentially, then, the replacement-level fertility rate, like the TFR, is an assumption-grounded prediction, and since demographic change usually occurs slowly in the human species, a human population will normally not become numerically flat in a short span of time. The human population of the world, in other words, will probably not reach a numerical plateau in the immediate future. The continuation of human-population growth may be surprising given the increase that has been occurring in the share of the world population that has a TFR no higher than its replacement-level fertility rate.[48] Such surprise, however, comes from an optimism that, regrettably, appears to be unwarranted.

1.3.3 Future numerical growth of the human population

As we have seen, the number of human beings who live on planet Earth has not stopped its upward climb, and the magnitude of the climb has been substantial. Figure 1.4 shows that additions to human-population size are likely to be large over the next several decades, too. Figure 1.4 is based on data from the United Nations Population Division and portrays world population growth over each ten-year interval from 2020 to 2050—intervals that are not far in the future and hence are reasonably predictable. The figure was developed using the estimate of world population size in 2020 and projections of future growth in the size of the population to the year 2050.[49] From the projections, I calculated the average yearly numerical increase in population that was forecast for the decade of 2020 to 2030, for the decade of 2030 to 2040, and for the decade of 2040 to 2050. The calculations for each decade employed three projections (or 'variants') of world population growth, viz., low, medium, and high.[50] Figure 1.4 graphs the results of the calculations. The bars in the inner region of the figure, together with the left vertical axis, show the mean number of people predicted to be added annually to the population of the world during the decade that precedes the year designated on the horizontal axis.

As Figure 1.4 makes plain, the forecasted yearly additions to the global population in coming decades are sizeable: Even though the magnitude of the additions will decrease, the human population will grow significantly. For example, during the last decade covered by the figure (that is, 2040 to 2050), the average yearly addition is predicted to be around 40,000,000 under the low-growth scenario, nearly 54,000,000 under the medium-growth scenario, and over 68,000,000 under the high-growth scenario.

The projections in Figure 1.4 involve large numbers of people, but might the projections be too high? The future is always subject to uncertainties, of course, and one that

Figure 1.4: Projected average yearly numerical increase of the human population: world, 2020 to 2030, 2030 to 2040, 2040 to 2050

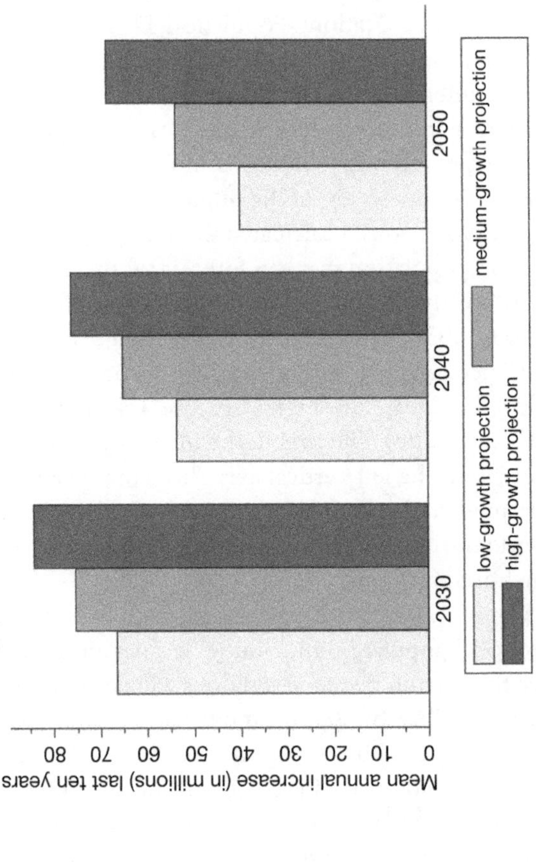

Source: Data from United Nations; calculations and graph by author (see note 49 in this chapter).

is pertinent here results from the ongoing COVID-19 pandemic.[51] The projected increases that are graphed in Figure 1.4 are derived from mid-year population sizes, and the last estimated (that is, as opposed to projected) mid-year population was for 2020,[52] shortly after the inception of the pandemic. Importantly, the vast majority of confirmed deaths attributed to COVID-19 happened subsequent to July 1, 2020[53] and thus might significantly reduce population growth in years after 2020. However, the increase in mortality due to the pandemic may be followed by a post-pandemic rise in fertility: The pandemic and its appreciable impact on human mortality[54] constitute a major, though presumably short-term, disruption of social life, and such a disruption may lead to an increase in childbearing.[55] An appreciably larger volume of disruption-caused childbearing can, in turn, have an impact on population size if this delayed childbearing more than makes up for the births that would have happened earlier, that is, is responsible for a final number of births per woman that exceeds the number that would have occurred in the absence of the pandemic.

1.4 A concluding comment

As Chapter Two elaborates, numerical additions to the population of *Homo sapiens* harm both the biosphere and human societies. The harms will not be prevented by an ostrich-like response to the situation, however, because even with innovations in technology and changes in consumption styles that reduce the biospheric effect of the average individual, humankind in the aggregate is outstripping the ability of the biosphere to provide for its needs. '[T]he overall condition of the global environment has continued to deteriorate' over the last two decades, the United Nations Environment Programme observed in 2019, and projected decreases in demand 'for key environmental resources … will be inadequate to reduce the pressure on already-stressed environmental systems.'[56] The extent to which demands have been placed on the environment is indicated by the emergence of efforts to mine minerals on objects in space (for example, asteroids),[57] but even mining in space appears unlikely to forestall problems other than shortages of (some) mineral resources. Based on available evidence, the problems are becoming more probable and their potential severity is increasing. They may, moreover, have no easy solutions. As a result, the problems may force human societies to decide between courses of action that differ only in the type and/or harshness of their negative repercussions. The human species, in short, is going beyond simple risk-taking; it is gambling and does not understand that gamblers must 'decide upon three things at the start: the rules of the game, the stake, and the quitting time.'[58] *Homo sapiens* is not in control of either the first or the second of these requisites, and seems unmindful of the third.

TWO

Impacts of Human Population Size and Growth: Recent Research

Elsewhere I have summarized a large body of evidence that ties the numerical size and growth of the population of *Homo sapiens* to a wide range of human-caused, negative effects on nature and the social life of people.[1] Simply put, the growing number of human beings, especially by expanding the amount of land devoted to urban areas, is placing ever-greater demands and stress on the biosphere.[2] In Chapter Two, I extend this body of evidence with additional studies of specific ways in which the biosphere and human societies have been injured by the increasing number of people on Earth. These studies are in line with recently published research that found the overall ecological footprint of the human species becomes larger as the number of human beings grows.[3] For example, a study covering 188 jurisdictions (nations and territories) during the years 1961 through 2016 concluded that the ecological footprint of the jurisdictions was made greater by additions to human-population density in the jurisdictions.[4]

2.1 COVID-19

I start my review with a subject on which I briefly touched earlier, viz., the COVID-19 pandemic.[5] Recent research has found that human-population density is positively related to the scale and severity of the COVID-19 outbreak — as population density went up, the COVID-19 pandemic worsened.

1. The basic reproduction number (R_0) for COVID-19, that is, the number of people in a susceptible population who were infected with COVID-19 by a single infected person, was the dependent variable in a study of 274 cities across the globe (but outside China) that had a population of not less than 500,000. With population size held constant, R_0 increased as population density rose. Population density, in other words, added to the number of infected people independently of population size (as well as, inter alia, the level of air pollution).[6]

2. Similarly, in a study of more than 150 nations worldwide, both higher population density and a larger proportion of the population that resided in an urban area were each found to raise the number of current active cases of COVID-19, with current active cases defined as the total number of cases after accounting for persons with COVID-19 who died or recovered from the disease. The impact of population density and the relative size of the urban population on the incidence of current cases was separate from the impact of, inter alia, the proportion of the population that was in the age range 65 and over.[7]

3. The rate of mortality from COVID-19 was the dependent variable in a study of 30 nations that had a population of 2,000,000 or more and a per-person gross domestic product of U.S. $27,000 or higher. The standardized regression coefficient for population density was positive and among the largest of the standardized regression coefficients for the independent variables in the study.[8]

The conclusions reached by the foregoing multi-nation studies are largely consistent with the conclusions reached by research on jurisdictions or geographic areas within a single nation: COVID-19 cases, this research finds, are more frequent in jurisdictions/areas that have greater population density and/or greater urbanization. Single-nation studies exist for China,[9] Great Britain,[10] India,[11] Turkey,[12] and the United States.[13]

2.2 Climate change

I next turn to the subject of climate change, which understandably has attracted a lot of attention and today may rank as the gravest immediate biospheric danger to *Homo sapiens*,[14] in part due to its deleterious effects on human health.[15] The change that the climate of the planet has undergone in recent times almost certainly is not natural variation; it is, instead, attributable to human beings and their activities.[16] Globally, temperatures have gone up and temperature extremes have become more common over the last six decades.[17] These trends are expected to persist, and with continued climate warming, severe heat waves will happen more often and affect a substantial portion of the world population.[18] In Europe and North America, heat waves have been increasing in frequency as well as intensity,[19] but the increases in Europe have generally exceeded the increases in North America.[20] In addition to this difference between continents, air temperatures differ between urban and non-urban areas since urbanization causes cities to have hotter air.[21] The number of people in urban areas of the planet who are exposed to high air temperatures is now large, therefore, with exposure generally increasing during recent decades because the human population in urban areas grew numerically.[22]

This background informs the review that I now undertake of four studies that deal with emissions of carbon dioxide into the atmosphere. Emissions of carbon dioxide are important because their increase has driven much of the industrialization-era rise in air temperatures over the land surface of the planet[23] and because the level of carbon dioxide in the atmosphere may not be reducible for centuries.[24]

The first of the four studies that I review utilized data covering almost six decades (1960 to 2018) on more than 150 nations; holding constant economic variables, the study found that total emissions of carbon dioxide were enlarged by growth in the number of people in the population and in urban areas of the nations.[25] The second study covered the period 1996–2018 and employed data on ten nations that had been part of the Soviet Union until its breakup in 1991. A multivariate analysis concluded that, with other factors held constant, per-person emissions of carbon dioxide became greater in response to increases in the yearly rate of population growth.[26] More carbon dioxide was emitted by the average individual in the ten nations, that is, as the pace at which nations added people became faster. In another study, data on China covering the years 1995–2018 revealed that, with other variables held constant, the numerical growth of the Chinese population was the agent most responsible for increasing carbon dioxide emissions.[27] A fourth study utilized state-level data on all U.S. states (rather than just the continental states) and concluded that states had higher emissions of carbon dioxide from the use of fossil fuels as, ceteris paribus, their populations grew larger.[28]

Quantitative research tells us, in short, that the growing number of human beings is a key reason for global increases of greenhouse gas emissions and the warming of the atmosphere.[29] Moreover, human population growth is a driver of urbanization,[30] and urban areas raise air temperatures.[31] Unsurprisingly, then, urban areas overall are hotter than vegetated land areas. In the United States, for example, urban areas are hotter than vegetated land areas by 1.9 degrees Centigrade (3.4 degrees Fahrenheit) in the summer and 1.5 degrees Centigrade (2.7 degrees Fahrenheit) in the winter.[32]

2.3 Cascading effects

Causal chains are not necessarily short, however, and they are lengthened when an effect has consequences of its own. In terms of climate change, the impact of human-population growth does not stop with atmospheric warming; the warming of the atmosphere has, in turn, brought about outcomes that are harmful to human societies. For example, the higher air temperatures involved in climate change have raised mortality rates and lowered life expectancy in nations where per-person income is less than the median per-person income for the world as a whole.[33] Additionally, climate warming has been responsible for enlarging the number of wildfires globally,[34] a trend that is not expected to end anytime soon; on the contrary, climate warming during the twenty-first century is projected to increase the exposure of the world to wildfires.[35] Importantly, the smoke from wildfires contains fine particulate matter that raises the incidence of death among human beings,[36] and wildfires of a severity that have not previously been seen on the planet may be generated in the future by climate change.[37] The United States may not escape these effects: The number and severity of wildfires in the United States in the middle of the twenty-first century may be greater than the yearly average during the period 1975 to 2005.[38]

Agriculture, too, is being and will be affected by climate change. A study of Europe that analyzed data covering more than 50 years found that climate change decreased the production of crops (especially cereals) through increased instances of severe weather such as droughts and heat waves.[39] Europe, however, is not the only region of the planet to have suffered.[40] The world as a whole has experienced, and in the future can be expected to experience, a range of significant effects on agriculture from more frequent severe weather events. These global effects include not just crop losses[41] but sizeable decreases in overall agricultural output relative to overall agricultural input[42] as well as reductions in overall economic activity. As to the economy, studies analyzing data that cover more than a half-century have concluded that global economic growth has already been curtailed by variations in air temperature,[43] an accompaniment of human-caused climate change.[44] Negative economic consequences can also be expected from climate change in the future[45] if, as is probable, the speed of climate change, and the variability and extremes of climate, increase during the twenty-first century.[46] Notably, reduced economic activity will likely be accompanied by greater economic damage to human societies from weather- and climate-related disasters since such damage has been mounting globally.[47]

Turning to an associated problem, meteorological models generally provide at least medium-to-high confidence that tropical cyclones (that is, hurricanes, and typhoons that develop over large tropical or subtropical bodies of water[48]) will be intensified, and the amount of rain they produce will be increased, by a human-caused 2° Centigrade warming of air temperatures,[49] a warming that is well within the realm of possibility.[50] The United States is thus projected to experience more severe coastal flooding from the hurricanes and sea-level rise that climate warming could produce in the late twenty-first century, with the severity of such flooding varying geographically, viz., being more severe in counties along the Gulf of Mexico and progressively less severe in counties higher in latitude along the U.S. East Coast.[51] In addition, climate change is increasing instances of abnormally high precipitation.[52] During July 2021, for example, severe flooding traceable to climate change occurred in Germany and the Benelux countries of Europe.[53] In the future, changes in climate are expected to increase substantially the number of people who experience floods. Thus, a simulation of floods in the continental United States over periods up to 200 years found that climate change and population growth will materially enlarge the number of people exposed to floods in the future.[54]

Oddly, more droughts are happening in the world concurrently with more floods as the result of atmospheric warming.[55] The increase in droughts is expected to continue. A simulation of evapotranspiration to the year 2100 concluded that the total number of people globally who will be exposed to extreme droughts will rise significantly; that climate change by itself will account for about three-fifths of the increase in exposure; that climate change in conjunction with population growth will be responsible for about one-third of the increase; and that population growth by itself will cause about one-tenth of the increase.[56]

The causal chain that originates with climate change, however, does not stop with floods and droughts. A notable example is that a drought in an area that is experiencing a heat wave may increase the temperature of the (already hot) air and worsen the drought.[57] The biosphere, that is, may be subject to and affected by feedback loops. Another example is that human beings may move geographically in response to droughts and floods, although droughts, which develop slowly, raise the frequency of migration more than floods, which occur rapidly.[58] Research has also concluded that, when weather-triggered migration happens, the migration is more likely to involve within-country moves across long distances than cross-country moves or within-country moves over short distances.[59] The social disruptions that weather-prompted migration causes in a nation are thus chiefly due to people who have traveled from relatively far places in the nation.

These findings of research on migration apply, of course, to migration in the past and hence may not apply in the remaining decades of the twenty-first century, when climate warming is expected to worsen. However, the findings are the best available guide to what will take place in the future, and they merit attention because during the twenty-first century, weather events around the world may prompt a vast number of people to migrate.[60] Naturally, the scale of this migration will be a function of, inter alia, the numerical size of the human population.

Before closing Chapter Two, a further point should be made: Human societies will be harmed simultaneously by climate change and by the loss of biodiversity. Both climate change and biodiversity loss need to be considered since each can affect the other—increases in atmospheric temperatures can reduce biodiversity,[61] and reductions in biodiversity can increase atmospheric warming.[62] Biodiversity loss is important to human societies because, inter alia, decreases in biodiversity seem to raise the frequency with which human beings are infected by disease-causing pathogens (including the 2019 novel coronavirus[63]) that can be transferred between vertebrate animals.[64] Unsurprisingly, the level of biodiversity is related inversely to the numerical size of the human population, that is, all else being equal, biodiversity diminishes as humans become more numerous.[65]

In multiple ways, then, environmental conditions that are harmful to the common good stem from the growth that has taken place in the number of human beings on the planet. Indeed, the numerical increase of the human population has become a 'threat multiplier,'[66] and in this regard, urbanization merits particular attention. With population growth, more people have taken up residence in cities, and the result has been that rates of human morbidity and mortality have gone up: Cities raise the frequency of microbe-caused illnesses[67] and increase atmospheric temperatures,[68] for example, and they generally produce higher rates of premature death from greater concentrations of fine particulate matter in the air.[69] Notably, the number of city residents is enlarged by climate problems.[70] Given that urbanization and climate change reinforce one another, the continued expansion of the human population can be expected to cause further harm to the biosphere and *Homo sapiens*.

THREE

Government Efforts to Change the Frequency of Childbearing and Immigration

Skepticism is prudent in all scholarly disciplines, including the social sciences, because error is always possible in scholarly work. Social scientists, therefore, may not reach the correct conclusion about whether the frequency of a societal activity is affected by an intervention such as law or government policy. Unsurprisingly, studies in the social sciences, as well as studies in the natural sciences, have reported findings as to cause-effect relationships that were not reproduced in follow-up research.[1]

Since the booby traps in quantitative research on law/policy effectiveness are not widely known, a pool of unwary consumers exists for the findings of flawed research. Notably, this pool includes persons concerned with the numerical size of the human population who believe that social science research has proven that the adoption and implementation of policies expanding the availability of family-planning methods bring about a relatively rapid and large diminution in human fertility and population growth. According to this belief, policies that promote access to family planning *on their own* materially lower the incidence of childbearing. For example, in a publication by a leading university-based school of public health in the United States, five former directors of the population and reproductive health program at the U.S. Agency for International Development contended that the provision of family-planning services in the past has cut the global rate of growth of the human population, that the magnitude of global population growth in years to come will 'depend[] largely upon future rates of contraceptive use,' and that the worldwide use of contraception will expand in the future only if the United States appreciably increases the assistance it provides internationally for family planning.[2] Their contention, moreover, was tied to empirical research: Studies of the impact of programs involving the 'community-based distribution' of family-planning methods and information, the authors wrote, have yielded 'impressive results in dozens of countries throughout the developing world' and have demonstrated a significant role for these programs in leading couples to rely on contraceptives.[3]

Are claims like these accurate? Can the numerical increase of *Homo sapiens* be materially reduced just by creating and expanding family-planning programs? The answer should begin with a brief overview of types of deficiencies that can lurk in research on law/policy effectiveness.

3.1 Social science methodology

When conducting research on the impact of law and government policy, a social scientist must be cognizant of a range of methodological pitfalls, because the failure to avoid even one of them may cause the social scientist to reach an erroneous conclusion. Let me mention and briefly explain eight such pitfalls.

First, a study of the impact of legislation or government policy must identify the precise point in time when the legislation/policy became active, that is, constituted a societal intervention. Notably, the date on which a statute or policy is adopted is often not, as a matter of law, the date on which the statute or policy is implementable, and the date on which a statute or policy is implementable may not be the date on which it is implemented. Indeed, a substantial amount of time may separate these dates. Consequently, when a statute or policy is officially 'on the books' may be much earlier than when it is enforceable, and when a statute or policy is enforceable may be much earlier than when it is enforced. Regrettably, however, a social scientist may mistakenly believe that one date represents a later date and hence rely on the former. In the United States, the dates may differ for a number of law-based reasons. For example, the dates may differ because the constitution of the jurisdiction that adopted the statute/policy, or a provision of the statute/policy itself, required the difference. The dates may differ also because, after the statute/policy was adopted, a court enjoined its enforcement in litigation that challenged the statute/policy, for example, litigation that questioned whether the statute/policy satisfied a provision of a constitution (federal or state). Additionally, the dates may differ because administrative-agency regulations for a statute/policy may have been needed. The regulations would have had to be formulated, and might have had to survive a challenge in court, before the statute/policy became enforceable.

Second, the numerical frequency of an activity after implementation of a statute or government policy may not deviate from the numerical frequency of the activity before the statute/policy was implemented. Similarly, the post-law/ post-policy rate of change in how often the activity occurred may not deviate from the pre-law/pre-policy rate of change in how often the activity occurred. The pre-law/pre-policy baseline, consequently, is key to identifying the direction and magnitude of an effect that a new law/policy had on the incidence of an activity. Moreover, data on the pre-law/pre-policy incidence of an activity must cover an extended period because a reliable baseline is required to ascertain whether the post-law/post-policy incidence deviated from the pre-law/ pre-policy incidence. Without a measurable deviation, the law/ policy cannot be said to have altered the incidence of the activity.

Third, a change in the frequency or rate of an activity after a new law/policy is implemented may not be due to the law/ policy. Instead, the post-law/post-policy change in frequency or rate may be due to macro-level forces that brought about the law/policy—forces that may be sociological, demographic, biospheric, and/or economic. When this happens, the law/policy is not the agent responsible for the post-law/post-policy change in how often the activity takes place. The cause of the change in frequency or rate is, rather, the macro-level forces that initiated the change and produced the new law/policy. The latter forces, however, may not have been measured by researchers, and studies that rely on data that omit the large-scale forces responsible for the new law/policy cannot trace the change in activity incidence to the forces, creating a problem known in social science as 'endogeneity.' As a result, research that seeks the determinants of the incidence of an activity and that suffers from endogeneity is precluded from accurately estimating the impact of law and government policy.[4]

A fourth pitfall is a corollary of the third. Specifically, the post-law/post-policy frequency or rate of an activity that is targeted by the law/policy may have changed not only in a jurisdiction that implemented the new law/policy (the treatment jurisdiction) but also in a jurisdiction that did not implement the law/policy but that is similar in other respects (the control jurisdiction). If the changes in activity incidence in the treatment jurisdiction and the control jurisdiction are in the same direction, are roughly the same in magnitude, and occur at roughly the same time, the new law/policy cannot be given credit for the post-law/post-policy change in incidence in the treatment jurisdiction. The change is, instead, due to an overarching event or force that affected both jurisdictions. For instance, following the introduction of new law/policy, human fertility may decline, but the decline may not be due to the law/policy; it may, instead, result from another factor, for example, hotter weather,[5] that affected the treatment jurisdiction and the control jurisdiction. Research on the impact of law/policy on a particular behavior, consequently, needs to include a control jurisdiction that, except for the presence of the law/policy, is similar to the treatment jurisdiction in all respects that have a bearing on the behavior.

Fifth, a new law/policy may bring about a sizeable change in the frequency or rate of the activity that the law/policy addresses, but the change may not last. Law/policy, in other words, may have a short-term (one- or two-year) impact that subsequently disappears. A short-term impact may be due, for example, to anticipation of the law/policy and its implementation. In this situation, the date on which the law/policy is expected to be implemented leads many people to postpone an action they are planning (for example, divorce) until after the law/policy is in force. A surge in the incidence of the action will thus occur after enforcement of the law/policy begins, but the surge will be followed by a decline (either gradual or rapid) in the incidence of the action, and eventually the post-law/post-policy incidence will match the pre-law/pre-policy incidence.

Sixth, new law/policy may produce a 'statistically significant' change in the frequency or rate of an activity, but a 'statistically significant' change means only that the change is unlikely to have occurred by chance in the sample that was studied if no change took place in the population from which the sample was drawn. Statistical significance, therefore, is not practical significance. Whether the magnitude of a statistically significant change is large and meaningful in practical terms is an entirely separate matter.[6]

Seventh, new law may reclassify the legality of an activity, shifting the status of the activity from lawful to unlawful or from unlawful to lawful. In order to evaluate accurately the effect of such law, research must measure the incidence of the activity when the activity is lawful *and* when it is unlawful. To illustrate, a new statute that bans an activity such as abortion or discrimination may not reduce how often the activity takes place; the activity may simply occur in violation of the statute. Therefore, to avoid reaching a wrong conclusion, a study of whether the statute altered the incidence of the activity must include data on the extent to which the activity happened illegally.

Eighth and finally, new law or policy may prompt persons engaged in a society-disfavored activity to move from one geographic area to another and continue the activity in the latter area;[7] alternatively, they may stay in the original geographic area and become involved in a different, and perhaps even less desirable, type of society-disfavored activity.[8] Given these possibilities, an accurate picture of the impact of a change in law/policy requires the study of all geographic areas and activity types that are potentially affected by the change.

The eight pitfalls listed here lead to a key point that should be kept in mind when dealing with social science research on agents that might alter the frequency or rate of a particular activity. Specifically, as the design of such research becomes more rigorous, the research becomes less likely to find that an agent has an effect on the targeted activity.[9] Conclusions that cause-effect relationships exist are thus not as credible when the conclusions are based on cross-sectional data as when they are based on longitudinal data. Causality involves a temporal interval between an agent and its effect, making longitudinal data more appropriate than cross-sectional data when studying whether an agent was responsible for what followed.

A further point to bear in mind is that exceptions to a generalization can exist, and although the vast majority of jurisdictions may not alter the frequency or rate of an activity through law or government policy, certain types of jurisdictions may do so. To illustrate, the law/policy of an island-nation may succeed in restricting immigration because the nation is surrounded by a body of water that serves as a natural barrier to immigration. The experience of the nation, however, is not necessarily generalizable to nations that have no such barrier.

3.2 Law and government policy on fertility

With the preceding background, we turn to empirical research that has investigated the effectiveness of law and government policy that was designed to alter how often individuals engage in certain types of society-significant social behavior. Importantly, this research offers scant comfort to proponents of using law and government policy to bring about a material, long-lasting change in the incidence of childbearing and immigration. At least in democracies, law and government policy that would logically be expected to influence the frequency and rate of childbearing and immigration have not been found to work well.[10] While law and government policy are evidently able to produce a substantial, permanent reduction in the environmentally damaging actions of entities,[11] they do not seem to have a marked, enduring impact on the incidence of participation by individuals in core societal activities. However, this limited impact should not be surprising; indeed, it is entirely understandable, as I contend in section 4.2 of *infra* Chapter Four.

To begin with childbearing, a review of multivariate research concluded that the effect on the incidence of births of fertility-supportive government policies 'tends to be small' and that the effect of these policies may be on when women bear children (that is, birth timing), not on how many children they bear.[12] Similarly, law and government policy that was designed to impede access to therapeutic abortion has not had a large, enduring impact on how often induced terminations of pregnancies occur in developed nations.[13] Due to data limitations,[14] the impact of such law/policy on the incidence of abortion in developing nations has not been adequately studied, but it is likely to be similar to the impact of family-planning programs in these nations. Let me therefore consider pertinent research on such programs.

Although family-planning programs would be expected to decrease childbearing, the available evidence (discussed next) indicates that they do not affect fertility to a substantial degree. I should note, however, that because the methodological pitfalls in research on the impact of law and government policy (*supra* section 3.1) are either not fully understood or not fully applied when evaluating studies of family-planning programs, advocacy of these programs continues with the prediction that implementation (or fuller implementation) of the programs will lead to much lower childbearing.[15] Unfortunately for the advocates, the prediction is unlikely to be proven correct and, instead, is likely to become another illustration of the principle that established ideas are frequently wrong. Certainly, the principle is seen in the history of science, where advances in knowledge often involve abandoning presently accepted ideas in favor of new ones.[16] The replacement of ideas, moreover, can be a bumpy process. As Albert Einstein pointed out more than a century ago,

> concepts that have proven useful in ordering things can easily attain an authority over us such that we ... take them as immutably given. They are then rather rubber-stamped as a 'sine-qua-non of thinking' and an 'a priori given,' etc. Such errors make the road of scientific progress often impassable for long times.[17]

Currently approved ideas, in short, can be mistaken, and should not prevent consideration of alternative ideas.

What is the evidentiary basis for doubting that family-planning programs materially dampen fertility? A summary of longitudinal research on the fertility impact of voluntary family-planning efforts in low-income and middle-income nations concluded that the fertility effects of the efforts 'vary substantially' and that the efforts 'may explain only about 4–20% of' the decrease in childbearing that took place; indeed, in three studies that were reviewed, the programs had no effect on the incidence of childbearing.[18] An examination of research on the fertility impact of organized family-planning efforts in 11 developing nations found that the efforts were 'inconsistent' in their impact on the frequency of childbearing; described the average fertility impact of the efforts as 'relatively small,' amounting to a reduction of just one-third of a child during the 30-year childbearing period of the average woman; and pointed out that in some studies a diminution in the availability of family planning was followed by lower fertility.[19]

Another study looked at 40 developing countries and estimated the impact on fertility in these countries of social-economic development level and family-planning program strength.[20] The study, which employed ordinary least-squares regression to analyze cross-sectional data for time points within the period 2003–2010, concluded that family-planning programs decreased childbearing,[21] but the magnitude of the effect of the programs could not be compared to the magnitude of the effect of social-economic development because the study relied entirely on, and reported only, unstandardized regression coefficients for its independent variables. A comparison of the impacts of two (or more) independent variables, however, requires standardized regression coefficients.

Fortunately, although the study (the 'Jain-Ross study') did not report standardized coefficients, it did provide, for all of the 40 countries it covered, the data that it used for every variable.[22] I was able, therefore, to repeat the statistical analysis of the study, that is, regress the total fertility rate (TFR) in each country on the numerical score for social-economic development in the country (measured by a three-factor Human Development Index or HDI), the numerical score for family-planning program strength (FPP) in the country, and a dummy variable for whether the country was located in sub-Saharan Africa (SSA). My regression analysis yielded the same unstandardized coefficients that the Jain-Ross study obtained for its variables and intercept.[23] Having gotten the same unstandardized coefficients, I estimated the standardized coefficients.[24]

The standardized coefficients that emerged from my regression of TFR on FPP, HDI, and SSA for the 40 countries were as follows:

Independent variable	Standardized coefficient
FPP	−0.208
HDI	−0.494
SSA	0.377

The standardized coefficients of interest here, of course, are those for FPP and HDI. Because each standardized coefficient is grounded on the standard deviation of not only its dependent variable but also on the standard deviation of its respective independent variable (rather than on the original numerical amount of the independent variable), the magnitude of one coefficient can be directly compared to the magnitude of another coefficient. Hence, these standardized coefficients show that an increase of one standard deviation in FPP decreased the TFR by .208 standard deviations, and an increase of one standard deviation in HDI decreased the TFR by 0.494 standard deviations. Since each effect is net of the other, the effect of HDI exceeded the effect of FPP by a ratio of 2.4 to 1 (-0.494 ÷ -0.208 = 2.4). Put differently, the standardized coefficients reveal that, in the 40 developing countries that were studied, the impact on fertility of social-economic development was comparatively large and that the impact on fertility of family-planning programs was comparatively small.

Let me close this review with a study of family-planning programs in the United States. The study concluded that the programs reduced U.S. births by approximately 1,800,000 during the ten years from 1964 through 1973.[25] Although this may seem to be a sizeable effect, live births in the United States totaled 35,698,000 over the ten-year period 1964–1973.[26] The family-planning programs, accordingly, were responsible for preventing

$$(1,800,000 \div (35,698,000 + 1,800,000)) =$$
$$1,800,000 \div 37,498,000 = .048 \times 100 = 4.8\%$$

of the births that would otherwise have happened in the United States during 1964–1973. Such an impact cannot, of course, be characterized as large.

What can we take away from the outlined studies? In brief, the creation and expansion of family-planning programs are responsible for relatively small reductions in childbearing. A substantial decline in fertility that occurs after a family-planning program becomes available in a nation is not chiefly attributable to the program per se but, instead, to broad social-economic change (including change in world views) brought about by society-level forces that generate a demand for contraception, sterilization, and abortion.[27] Said otherwise, family-planning programs arise and spread in a society as part of a society-level process that reshapes the society in ways that reduce the number of children wanted by reproductive-age individuals. The establishment of family-planning programs thus answers a societal call that stems from macro-level social and economic change, with the movement toward lower fertility in a society pushed much less by the former (family-planning programs) than by the latter (social and economic change).

Perhaps surprisingly, the primacy of social-economic change in the transition to lower fertility is implicit in what advocates of population control say when pressing for the adoption and expansion of family-planning programs. In particular, their message emphasizes that, to decrease fertility permanently, family-planning methods must be used voluntarily; if use of the methods is coerced, employment of the methods will not last.[28] Family-planning methods cannot avert pregnancies and births unless they are employed, of course, and family-planning proponents point out that the methods will be employed over a prolonged period only if utilization of the methods is voluntary. However, that family planning must be voluntary means that family planning must be acceptable to its users, that is, must align with what is socially approved and desired. Social approval and desirability, in turn, depend on and vary with current social-economic conditions—conditions that are molded by macrosociological and macroeconomic forces. As a result, the message of family-planning advocates contains an implicit acknowledgment that the character of a society and the causal agents responsible for this character determine whether a family-planning program develops in the society and whether reduced childbearing follows.

Let me take a further step in analyzing the family-planning message. Specifically, the social-economic conditions that form the character of a society include the family-size goals of the members of the society, which goals establish not just when births are wanted but also when births are not wanted. Obviously, family-planning methods are directed at and are utilized to prevent the occurrence of *unwanted* pregnancies and births.[29] This purpose, however, takes us back to the point that family-planning methods and the organized family-planning programs that supply them will not be accepted in a society unless they are compatible with the existing social milieu. The compatibility of family-planning programs with their social context, and particularly with dominant family-size goals, has a significant implication—the compatibility means that the programs will not actively and substantially change the number of births that individuals of childbearing age want to have.[30] Family-planning methods and programs, in other words, fit into the existing social order, because if they seriously disturbed it, they would be unable to obtain and expand a foothold in the society. Expressed more simply, the availability of and reliance on family-planning methods stem from a societal need to prevent unwanted pregnancies and births, a need produced by macro-level forces that have reshaped social-economic conditions in ways that have caused many potential pregnancies and births to be not wanted by individuals who are able to reproduce.[31]

In closing section 3.2, a few general comments may be helpful. When attempting to ascertain the impact of family-planning programs on the incidence of childbearing in countries, social scientists must quantify and statistically control the social-economic development level of the countries. However, the manner in which social-economic development level is measured remains unsettled,[32] and the definition of social-economic development has not been constant over time.[33] The uncertainty and fluidity of the concept of social-economic development must not be ignored when considering studies of family-planning programs because differences in the way in which social-economic development is measured may lead to non-trivial inconsistencies in multivariate estimates of the fertility impact of the programs. Furthermore, studies of the fertility impact of family-planning programs need to take into account differences in culture, not just differences in social-economic development. Fertility is affected by culture per se,[34] probably in part because culture molds the beliefs that exist in religion[35] and religions are not uniform in their teachings on family planning.[36] Erroneous conclusions can thus be drawn by researchers who fail to include data on and a control for culture when ascertaining what family-planning programs accomplish with respect to fertility rates.

3.3 A further look at the dispute over the fertility impact of family-planning programs

The family-planning movement has garnered widespread social approval, and deservedly so. However, as I pointed out in section 3.2, firm evidentiary support is lacking for the claim often made by the movement that the incidence of childbearing is materially reduced by and because of the availability of family-planning programs. In completing the instant book, however, I was directed to two papers that were offered as support for the claim of the family-planning movement. I review the papers here.

Of the two papers, one is labeled a 'discussion paper' and summarizes evidence from a variety of sources to back its contention that the distribution of family planning is the chief cause of falling fertility rates.[37] The most relevant of the sources that are cited relies on graphs of sets of nations. Although differences exist between the sets in the presence and strength of family-planning programs, the graphs do not rigorously assess whether, and by how much, country total fertility rates react to family-planning programs independently of social-economic change. To estimate the magnitude of the impact of the programs on the incidence of childbearing, a multivariate analysis of data would be required.

Turning to the second paper, the author, as support for the position that family-planning programs substantially decrease childbearing, references a book whose chapters cover family-planning programs in 23 jurisdictions.[38] The last chapter of the book (the 'Robinson-Ross chapter') brings together these jurisdictions in a statistical analysis concerned with whether the family-planning programs had an impact on the total fertility rate (TFR) of the jurisdictions during the period 1970–1975. In jurisdictions of less than 'high' social-economic development, the TFR was found to vary inversely with family-planning program strength. Specifically, the TFR in these jurisdictions was lower when the strength of their family-planning programs was 'moderate' than when it was 'weak.'[39]

Unfortunately, the study in the Robinson-Ross chapter only mentions a multivariate regression analysis, and does not provide the detailed results of the analysis. Instead, the chapter reports the mean TFR for each of the nine categories that resulted from crossing (i) three ordinally scaled groups of jurisdictions that, during 1970–1975, differed in social-economic level ('high,' 'middle,' and 'low') and (ii) three ordinally scaled groups of jurisdictions that, during the same period, differed in family-planning program strength ('strong,' 'moderate,' and 'weak'). Notably, three of the nine cells in the resulting 3 x 3 table contained no jurisdictions, and one of the nine cells contained just a single jurisdiction. Moreover, all of the levels of social-economic development were represented by the three cells that were without any jurisdictions. The findings reported in the Robinson-Ross chapter, consequently, are based on an imprecise and incomplete control for social-economic development.

More credible, though still not definitive, evidence regarding the effect of family-planning programs on the incidence of fertility would be obtained from regressing the 1970–1975 TFR in all of the 23 jurisdictions on quantitative indicators, measured with ratio scales or interval scales,[40] of the strength of family-planning programs and the level of social-economic development in the jurisdictions in 1970–1975. A regression analysis that included ratio- or interval-scale indicators for these independent variables would more fully remove the influence of social-economic factors on the TFR and more accurately gauge the relationship between family-planning program strength and the TFR. Readers should keep in mind, however, that such an analysis would be relying on cross-sectional data and that cross-sectional data are less appropriate than longitudinal data for establishing whether, and the degree to which, family-planning programs alter the TFR independently of social-economic level. Furthermore, the analysis would be using data for a relatively small number of jurisdictions. These jurisdictions, of course, may in important ways be unlike the many jurisdictions that are not in the data. Additionally, the limited number of jurisdictions in the analysis permits just one jurisdiction to create appreciable bias in the regression coefficients. If bias is present, the outlier responsible for it would need to be identified and removed from the data before running the final regression analysis.

Let me turn now to a study cited in the Robinson-Ross chapter, because it reported what that chapter did not. The cited study analyzed data on 78 developing nations for the 1980–1985 period and estimated that, in these nations, family-planning programs reduced the TFR by 1.2 births per woman,[41] a change that amounts to a program-induced decrease in the TFR of approximately 22 per cent. The estimate stemmed from a calculation that was based on the application of multivariate regression to cross-sectional data.[42]

An aspect of the cited study merits special attention. Family-planning program strength in the studied nations was measured by a four-factor index on which a nation could have a numerical score ranging from a minimum of 0 to a maximum of 120.[43] The regression coefficient for the index was not statistically significant at or below a probability of .05, meaning that program strength per se had no effect on the TFR. The coefficient for social-economic development, on the other hand, was statistically significant and negative.[44] The two coefficients tell us that increments in program strength did not affect the TFR when social-economic development level was zero but that increments in social-economic development level depressed the TFR when program strength was zero.[45] Because the magnitude of one independent variable was allowed to fluctuate while the magnitude of the other independent variable was held constant, these coefficients reveal the degree to which each variable on its own affected fertility.

The regression analysis, however, also included a variable for the *interaction* of family-planning program strength and social-economic development. The coefficient for the interaction variable was statistically significant (at a probability of .01) and negative. If the program-strength variable is labeled x and the development-level variable is labeled z, the numerical value of the coefficient for the interaction variable (that is, for xz) reveals the amount of alteration in the *effect* on the TFR caused by one of the independent variables (for example, x) when the other independent variable (for example, z) rises a single measurement unit. The sign of the coefficient for xz shows the direction in which the dependent variable (labeled y) is moved. Expressed differently, the coefficient for the interaction variable xz discloses what a one-unit increase in *either* x or z does to the impact on the dependent variable of a one-unit increase in the *other*.

The coefficient [for the interaction variable] indicates by how much the effect of x on y changes per unit increase in z. It also indicates the logically and mathematically identical amount by which a unit increase in x changes the effect of z on y. Neither is precisely an effect. They are statements of how an effect *changes*: that is, an effect on an effect.[46]

Does this discussion allow a conclusion to be drawn from the cited study as to whether the key determinant of fertility is social-economic development or family-planning programs? In seeking an answer, I rely on a pair of considerations. The first is the finding by the study that the response of the TFR was statistically related (inversely) to development level and was unrelated to program strength.[47] These findings must be interpreted, of course, in light of the statistically significant (and negative) coefficient for the interaction variable. One interpretation is that greater social-economic development can convert the statistically insignificant coefficient for program strength into a statistically significant (negative) coefficient, that is, can transform family-planning programs from an ineffective tool into an effective tool for lowering fertility. Such a transformation, if it were to happen, would suggest that the TFR is driven down chiefly by advances in social-economic conditions, and since the regression coefficient for program strength is far from the probability that warrants rejection of the null hypothesis,[48] social-economic advances would necessarily be a very powerful agent affecting fertility.

The second consideration is theory because theory cannot be divorced from the search for and interpretation of statistical interaction.[49] The coefficient for the interaction variable in the study can be construed as suggesting that greater family-planning program strength adds to the effect that social-economic development has on the TFR. Such an interpretation is attractive under structural-functionalism theory,[50] the sociological theory that (with some modification) informs the present book. Structural-functionalism theory deals with overarching societal forces, and would deem social-economic development, but not family-planning programs, to be such a force. Structural-functionalism theory, therefore, supports the inference from the coefficient for the interaction variable that the critical macro-level driver of the TFR is social-economic development and that family-planning programs are a helpful byproduct of social-economic development.

3.4 Law and government policy on immigration

Is the volume of immigration more responsive to law and government policy than the volume of births? Research suggests that the answer is negative and that the volume of immigration is largely unaffected by government regulation. Perhaps not surprisingly, governmental measures that were adopted to limit immigration into the United States have been subjected to considerable social science scrutiny. The evidence from this scrutiny, however, is not encouraging to advocates and backers of the measures—the effectiveness of the measures in curtailing immigration has been found to be, in a word, wanting.[51] Even efforts to deter immigration into relatively compact geographic areas of the country have proven unsuccessful: City governments in the United States that adopted policies unfavorable to immigrants were found not to have smaller foreign-born or Hispanic foreign-born populations than city governments that adopted policies favorable to immigrants.[52] Anti-immigration policies of U.S. cities thus did not reduce, and pro-immigration policies of U.S. cities did not increase, the presence of persons who were born outside the United States, including persons of Hispanic ethnicity.

The United States, however, is not unique in its inability to dampen the incidence of immigration substantially through government regulation. Research on the immigration policies of nations worldwide suggests that (1) the effectiveness of such policies is circumscribed by 'powerful structural migration determinants,' that is, by social, economic, and demographic conditions; and (2) because of unintended policy effects, such policies, while decreasing the number of immigrants who arrive in a country, can also decrease the number of immigrants who after arrival leave the country.[53] Immigration policies, accordingly, do not necessarily alter the net rate of migration experienced by a nation or the number of immigrants who reside in the nation. Thus, a review of research concluded that the immigration policies of nations have had a larger impact on 'the [place of] origin and internal composition of migration ... than [on] the overall volume and long-term trends of migration.'[54]

FOUR

The Concept of a System: Ecology, Sociology, and the Social Side Effects of Law/Policy

Do the studies reviewed in Chapter Three mean that law and government policy cannot contribute to stopping population growth? In order to answer this question, I must take a detour. I return to the question later in Chapter Four.

4.1 Ecology and sociology

The biology-based discipline of ecology focuses on the connections that exist among living organisms and between these organisms and their physical surroundings.[1] Being a branch of biological science, ecology does not concentrate on human societies and the social forces that determine the character of human societies. Instead, the social sciences, particularly the discipline of sociology, have the responsibility for studying how human societies are structured and how they work. Simply put, ecologists and sociologists follow very different paths, and each group is unfamiliar with the key ideas of the other.[2] Even the field known as human ecology, which has had footholds in both ecology and sociology and possesses the ability to bring these disciplines together,[3] has been unable to meld the two disciplines[4] since its founding in the first half of the twentieth century.[5]

Of course, the placement of ecology and sociology in distinct fields of scientific endeavor is not without a logical foundation, but the separation of ecology from sociology must also be seen as an artifact of history. The phenomena that a scientific discipline investigates are not prepackaged and neatly presorted. Rather, the disciplines of science and their boundaries are human constructs; the phenomena on which each discipline focuses have been assigned by scientists.[6] Unfortunately, however, the allocation of ecology and sociology to different, indeed distant, spheres is not just unnecessary; it may also be harmful. In terms of population–biosphere connections, the allocation is likely to be dissuading ecologists and sociologists from collaborating with one another (as well as with social scientists who are not sociologists[7]) in efforts to understand the effects of human societies on the biosphere and the effects of the biosphere on human societies. More ecology-sociology interaction would be beneficial because sociology has tools to offer that can improve studies of the biological-physical aspects of the planet that is home to *Homo sapiens*.[8]

Although disciplines are the main source of differentiation within science,[9] the presence of disciplines is not an absolute bar to interdisciplinary mixing and the emergence of a new specialty—the wall placed between two disciplines can slow down but cannot prevent the development of a hybrid that will be beneficial. Indeed, new hybrids have emerged over time in science.[10] Notably, dangers to the human species that are present in its environment have been an important reason for changes and advances in science.[11] Certainly, the state of the biosphere today ought to provide an impetus for new directions in science.

4.2 The concept of a system

A first step toward a collaboration between ecology and sociology may involve recognizing that the two disciplines share a concept that is important to both, namely, the concept of *system*. As a prominent American educator once observed, 'an intellectual community' requires 'a common language, [and] a common stock of ideas,' but its development is inhibited by specialization.[12] Since concepts are part of the language of science, the concept of a system provides ecologists and sociologists with a basis for understanding one another.[13]

Simply defined, a system is a phenomenon whose parts are interrelated and influence one another.[14] Given these attributes, a system is a whole that is more than the sum of its parts. The idea of a system is inherent in ecology because ecology often focuses on ecosystems.[15] The idea of a system is inherent in sociology, too, because sociology (or at least macrosociology) focuses on human societies and every human society is considered to be a system rather than an assemblage of unconnected individuals. If the increases in the population of *Homo sapiens* that are being produced by human societies are to be brought to an end by non-Malthusian means, we should appreciate the system character of society as well as the system character of the biosphere.[16]

A bridge, then, is possible between sociology and ecology as scientific disciplines. That bridge may be furnished by the idea of a 'social-ecological system'[17] or, perhaps, the idea of a 'societal-biosphere system.'[18] In terms of human overpopulation, the foregoing ideas are alike in underscoring a pair of principles: (1) the numerical size of societies of *Homo sapiens* affects the scale of human activities, and (2) since human beings engage with their environment, the scale of human activities affects the state of the world. The conclusion—that growth in the number of people raises the level of human activities and reduces the well-being of the biosphere—is backed by a wealth of credible evidence.[19] Moreover, the number of people on Earth may damage the biosphere of the planet by acting not alone but, rather, in concert with other environmental factors and hence by creating synergies.[20] If and where synergies happen, the effects that societies of *Homo sapiens* have on the biosphere can be multiplicative, not merely additive.

Let me deal now with the question of why the system aspect of human society must be taken into account when seeking interventions such as law and government policies that may reduce or halt growth in the number of people. The answer to the question begins with the macrosociological principle that a human society, being a system, has a propensity for internal integration.[21] Alternatively expressed, a human society inherently tends to defend against disintegration and, in so doing, acts to promote its continuation. A society of human beings, therefore, is concerned with maintaining what presently exists and resistant to a major shift in direction and/or rate of change. Since this resistance involves the very character of a society as a system, law and policy are able to have just small impacts on the volume of childbearing and immigration. Moreover, we should keep in mind that societal integration is a prerequisite to societal effectiveness—ceteris paribus, a society that is well-integrated operates more effectively than a society that is not—and a society will normally favor effectiveness over ineffectiveness.[22] To offer an example, trust is a component of social integration[23] and contributes to the ability of a society to deal with outbreaks of disease. In particular, a society characterized by a high level of trust has a better chance of minimizing the severity of an outbreak than a society characterized by a low level of trust.[24]

Nonetheless, the resistance of a human society to making adjustments to changed circumstances means that the society can, for a while, behave in ways that are inimical to its own interests. An instance is found in Figure 1.1—human societies have been and are harming the biosphere even though they cannot in the long run survive, let alone thrive, without the services that a well-functioning biosphere supplies.[25] Eventually, of course, a society engaged in ill-considered actions will come under pressure to end these actions because it cannot last and prosper unless it does so. However, because human societies are systems and protect their internal integration, they do not immediately alter course. Human societies today, therefore, are not moving quickly to reduce the growth of the human population and the negative impact of this growth on the biosphere.

Societal resistance to a shift in course, we should not forget, is a theoretical concept and cannot be directly observed. Societal resistance must thus be measured through manifested visible outcomes. Such outcomes include, inter alia, society-level actions that neutralize interventions and/or that redirect interventions away from their intended targets. Societal resistance can logically result, too, in outcomes that are unwanted, that is, side effects. Side effects are possible because a human society is a system and a system can respond in unanticipated, even counterproductive, ways when subjected to an intervention like the adoption or removal of a particular proscription or prescription of law. Unfortunately, however, sociology knows relatively little at the moment about the social side effects of law, but these effects may be important and may occur often.[26] Consequently, potential solutions to overpopulation must be accompanied by the conscious realization that every proposed solution carries the risk that it will not work, or may even worsen matters. Simply said, the law of unintended consequences, as it is popularly known, may operate and lay waste to an otherwise attractive approach to overpopulation.

4.3 Social side effects of law/policy

In section 4.3, I offer two case studies that illustrate social side effects that have resulted from the introduction of new law. Because the case studies involve law that had different objectives and come from societies that are sociologically dissimilar, they suggest that law-generated social side effects are not uncommon. Ecologically, as biologist Garrett Hardin observed, 'we can never do merely one thing.'[27] Sociologically, too, we cannot change just one thing.

The first case study is the policy that the government of China adopted in 1979 to curtail domestic population growth by imposing a one-birth maximum on each Chinese woman who belonged to the majority (Han) ethnic group.[28] The policy, which lasted in excess of 30 years[29] and may represent 'the largest social experiment in human history,'[30] surprisingly made an uncertain contribution to lowering the level of childbearing in China.[31] However, while the policy may not have appreciably dampened childbearing, it did have social side effects—the policy substantially raised the sex ratio (the number of males per 100 females)[32] and materially increased the aggregate crime rate.[33] In addition, the policy affected Chinese society by (1) altering the marriage rate and marriage partners selected;[34] (2) increasing the incidence of crimes committed by females;[35] (3) promoting direct, between-family private adoptions of children whose birth had put the biological parents over the one-child maximum;[36] and (4) causing the desertion, relinquishment, and stealing of children.[37] The policy, in short, did not escape the law of unintended consequences.[38]

The second case study comes from the United States and involves the federal Voting Rights Act of 1965.[39] The aim of the Act was to prevent government from discriminating on the basis of race in determining which U.S. citizens are qualified to cast a ballot in elections.[40] As an illustration of the social side effects of law, the Act is important because it has been ranked at the pinnacle of U.S. civil rights statutes and acclaimed for its role in combatting discrimination in suffrage against members of racial groups who resided in jurisdictions where such discrimination was at its worst.[41] However, while the Act has been described as 'a momentous achievement,'[42] did it substantially improve the position of racial minorities in American political affairs? Given the widespread assumption that law ameliorates social problems, a positive answer to the question would be anticipated. However, as I explain in detail elsewhere,[43] credible evidence exists to conclude that the Act, through the social stress that it produced, was probably responsible for a *reduction* in the ability of the black population living in southern U.S. states (the main target of the Act) to sway election outcomes. The likely reduction occurred because, in response to the Act, many more whites than blacks registered to vote.

4.4 Law, policy, and fertility

The number of people in a population is a function of three demographic factors, namely, fertility, mortality, and migration (immigration and emigration). For the population of the world as a whole, however, migration is irrelevant because the geographic movement of people does not alter the total number of people on the planet. I focus on fertility rather than mortality since my interest is in the number of people joining the global population, not the number of people leaving it.[44] I thus consider law and government policy that might curtail fertility.

A point that warrants mention is that even if law and government policy that openly and primarily seeks to reduce childbearing did not produce side effects, this type of law/policy is unlikely to be adopted by democracies in the near future. Law/policy that expressly aims to dampen childbearing will encounter strong public opposition because it is in sharp conflict with widely held social values. Current values emphasize the personal rights and dignity of the individual over the welfare of society;[45] in the United States, they also favor satisfying short-term desires over meeting long-term needs.[46] These social values—which, unsurprisingly, are embedded in features of the personalities of individuals[47]—create a roadblock to government action that is explicitly designed to curtail human fertility.

4.5 A proposal

Nonetheless, law and government policy may furnish a path to a sustained lower level of childbearing in the human species. Recognizing that law/policy has side effects, we should anticipate that government action whose express goal is *not* to affect the frequency of childbearing may nonetheless bring about lower fertility. To do so, law/policy will have to be in line with and facilitate a fertility-related trend that already exists. Law/policy is unlikely to stop, reverse, or redirect such a trend, because as a component of a system, it must work with, not against, societal conditions and the direction in which social life is moving.[48]

Section 4.5 describes and explains a proposal for such law/ policy. In introducing the proposal, I must emphasize that additional proposals should be developed by environmentally oriented scholars and that each of the proposals should be evaluated quantitatively by social scientists. Numerous proposals ought to be considered because not all law/policy will be equally practical and efficacious; proposals other than mine could well be more attractive and hold more promise for decreasing fertility. Let me also emphasize that my proposal does not imply that organized family-planning programs should be abandoned or even that they should be given less than full funding. Although these programs do not materially lower fertility on their own, they meet a demand for fertility-preventing resources and can contribute to a reduction in childbearing.[49]

With the foregoing in mind, let me suggest that urban planning that raises population density in residential housing is likely to curtail the number of births.[50] Of note in this regard is that higher density in housing is in line with a current push in urban planning to increase housing density.[51] Further, raising the level of density in housing through urban planning can do more than depress fertility: In raising population density in housing, urban planning can curtail per-capita energy consumption[52] and lower emissions of carbon dioxide.[53] These objectives align with the goals of environmentalists. However, to safeguard the functioning of the biosphere, urban planning will be required to promote the presence of trees[54] and overcome the reduced amount of space devoted to trees and other vegetation that accompanies higher residential density.[55] It will also need to prevent an elevation of the risk of person-to-person transmission of disease-causing agents in housing with higher densities. This will be required not just to avoid illness[56] but also to promote the acceptance of high-density housing.[57]

Even without interventions by urban planners, of course, housing density will increase as human beings become more numerous, but urban planning can maximize the commonweal in responding to and curbing growth in the size of the human population. Unfortunately, higher population density in housing, whether or not planned, will make housing space more expensive because population growth adds to housing prices;[58] indeed, the rate of increase in the price of residential housing in a geographic area surpasses the rate of increase in the numerical size of the human population in the area.[59] The higher housing prices are not, however, due to urban planning per se. The greater cost of housing is, rather, the result of the growth that has occurred in the number of human beings and that has made urban planning necessary.

I close Chapter Four with an important point regarding urban planning (and, indeed, other policies that may decrease childbearing). To be most effective in curbing fertility, policymakers must be aware of, and incorporate into what they design, several demographic variables. These variables can be abstruse to persons who lack expertise in demography. In the next chapter, consequently, I explain the variables and review the statistical measures for them.

FIVE

Fertility Rates, Mean Age
of Childbearing, and Childlessness

As explained earlier,[1] the total fertility rate (TFR) is a projection, for a particular year, of the average number of live births that females aged 15 in that year will have as they go through the age range (that is, 15–49) in which females are assumed to be physically capable of childbearing. The TFR is computed by using, or more exactly by summing, all of the age-specific fertility rates that prevailed in the year for which the TFR is calculated, but age-specific fertility rates have utility beyond their contribution to the TFR. To be exact, age-specific fertility rates can reveal (1) the relative level of fertility among females at different ages and (2) whether temporal trends in fertility at the various ages are similar to or differ markedly from one another. The insights gleaned from (1) can inform efforts to modify fertility rates by directing attention to the ages that are the source of the largest numbers of births. These insights can be supplemented by the information gleaned from (2), which allows identification of the ages that over time have been experiencing relatively rapid changes in fertility. The fertility of females at a given age will shift by a greater absolute amount, or will shift at a quicker pace, than the fertility of females at another age to the degree that fertility at the former age is affected by the macro-level forces that influence fertility in a society. When that happens—when fertility at certain ages is changing more than fertility at other ages—some ages can be ranked higher in efforts to alter levels of fertility, with the choice based on the relative contribution that each age makes to overall childbearing. For example, an age that produces fewer births than another age and is undergoing a slower decline in fertility than the other age could be assigned a lower priority, because the lower-priority age has less potential, all else being equal, to contribute to an aggregate reduction in future births. The information derived from both (1) and (2), therefore, can aid in formulating measures that may affect the numerical growth of the population.

5.1 Age-specific fertility rates

Since the total fertility rate of the world is not the only way to probe shifts in global childbearing levels for the purpose of understanding historical change in the number of human beings on Earth, I consider rates of fertility among females at the ages that have produced the overwhelming share of all births. Aggregating the 14 five-year intervals from 1950–1955 to 2015–2020, Table 5.1 reports, by the age of females in their childbearing years (column 1), the percentage (column 2) that females at a given age contributed to the TFR of the world as a whole during this time; cumulative percentages were tallied from the percentages in column 2 and are shown in column 3. Five ages had fertility rates that accounted for at least 5.0 percent of the global TFR in the period 1950–1955 to 2015–2020. They were 15–19, 20–24, 25–29, 30–34, and 35–39. In combination, these five ages were responsible for more than nine-tenths of the yearly global TFR, as seen in the last column of the table.[2]

Figure 5.1 was constructed in light of the preceding.[3] The figure graphs the fertility rates of each of the five ages responsible for 5.0 percent or more of the global TFR across the 14 five-year intervals covered by the figure. A brief explanation of Figure 5.1 may be helpful. The horizontal axis specifies the beginning year of each of the 14 five-year

Table 5.1: Mean contribution to the world total fertility rate of each age in the childbearing period of females since the mid-twentieth century

Column 1 (age of female)	Column 2 (% of TFR)	Column 3 (cumulative %)
15–19	9.3	9.3
20–24	27.2	36.5
25–29	27.2	63.7
30–34	19.1	82.8
35–39	11.2	94.0
40–44	4.8	98.8
45–49	1.2	100.0

intervals, with the inner region of the graph showing the age-specific fertility rates for the *midpoints* of the intervals. Thus, 1950 on the horizontal axis represents 1950–1955, at the midpoint of which the fertility rate of females aged 15–19 was 432.5 and the fertility rate of females aged 20–24 was 1173.5. Each five-year interval ends at the midpoint of the next interval on the axis. The last year on the horizontal axis, that is, 2015, marks the midpoint of the five-year interval that ran from mid-2015 to mid-2020.

Figure 5.1 offers statistical evidence backing a common observation, viz., that women in their twenties are the largest source of births, and it also brings out what could be expected from Figure 1.3, viz., that women in their twenties experienced sizeable declines in fertility. However, Figure 5.1 makes plain what Figure 1.3 does not, viz., that the fertility declines among women aged 20–24 were remarkably similar to the fertility declines among women aged 25–29. Women in their twenties, accordingly, have evidently been responsive to the macro-level forces that have been curbing the overall incidence of births, suggesting that the fertility of these women will also be responsive to urban planning that raises population density in housing. But there is an additional reason for policymakers to focus on women in their twenties. I discuss this reason next.

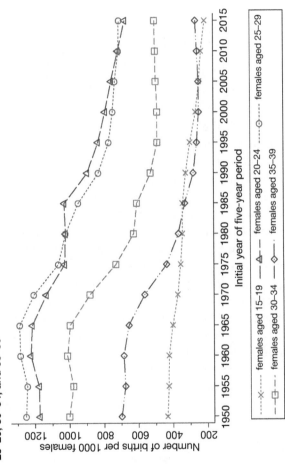

Figure 5.1: Fertility rates since the mid-twentieth century: world, females aged 15–19, 20–24, 25–29, 30–34, and 35–39

Source: See note 3 in this chapter.

5.2 Mean age of childbearing among women

The average age of childbearing among women who bear children is a major variable affecting fertility rates and, hence, change in the numerical size of the human population.[4] Simple arithmetic explains the impact of the variable: Among mothers, an average childbearing age of 25.0 years produces four generations of children over the course of a century while an average childbearing age of 33.3 years yields just three generations. As the illustration indicates, population growth will, ceteris paribus, decelerate when the female average age of childbearing goes up and will accelerate when the female average age of childbearing goes down. Notably, upward movements in the female average age of childbearing can do more than just reduce the aggregate number of births during a time interval—by curtailing births, increases in the average childbearing age among females can improve the physical health of women.[5]

The latter point leads us back to urban planning. Given the evidence that the frequency of health problems among mothers is lowest when mothers wait until they age into their early to mid-thirties before starting to bear children,[6] urban planning will materially benefit women, in the course of reducing the number of births in the human species, by moving the female average age of childbearing into that age range, that is, the early to mid-thirties, and discouraging fertility among women outside of it. Since a very large share of all births worldwide during recent decades has been to females who were in their twenties, as seen in Table 5.1 and Figure 5.1, these females are especially able to raise the global female average age of childbearing. Females who are younger than age 20 are less able to do so given their comparatively small contribution to the TFR, but even if reduced childbearing among females who are yet to celebrate their twentieth birthday does little to the female average age of childbearing, a reduction in their fertility will be beneficial. To be specific, childbearing by females before age 20 carries an elevated risk of birth defects, and since childbearing at or after age 40 does, too,[7] the societal interest in curbing population growth and improving public health makes the early to mid-thirties the age range within which the female average age of childbearing should fall and the overwhelming majority of births should occur.

What has been the global female average age of childbearing, and what if any change has taken place in it? The question is answered in Figure 5.2,[8] which presents estimates of the female average age of childbearing age over the 14 five-year periods from 1950–1955 to 2015–2020.[9] The estimates are both for all nations, that is, the world as a whole, and for groups of nations defined by their income level. Three income levels—high, middle, and low—are used. Each level is measured in terms of gross national income per capita expressed in U.S. dollars and covers a range.[10] In the current (fiscal year 2022) classification of nations by income level, the range for high-income nations is U.S. $12,696 and above; the range for middle-income nations runs from U.S. $1,046 to U.S. $12,695; and the range for low-income nations is U.S. $1,045 and below.[11] Income levels are useful because they are linked to the biospheric impact of *Homo sapiens*. Simply put, as nations become wealthier, their negative environmental impact tends to go up despite their enhanced ability to lessen this impact.[12]

Readers will notice in Figure 5.2 that, as in the prior figure, the horizontal axis designates the first year of a five-year period. The year 1950 thus marks the five-year period from mid-1950 to mid-1955 while the year 2015 marks the five-year period from mid-2015 to mid-2020.

What do we learn from Figure 5.2? Among high-income nations, the average age bottomed during 1975–1980 and then rose rapidly, adding slightly more than three years over the next four decades. During the last period (2015–2020), the average age was 30.2 years in high-income nations, and there was no indication that its rise was about to end. Among middle-income nations, the average age reached its lowest point

(27.3 years) during 1995–2000, that is, 20 years later than in high-income nations. Furthermore, although middle-income nations subsequently experienced an increase in the female average age of childbearing, the increase was just a half-year, reaching 27.8 years during 2015–2020. Among low-income nations, the average age remained steady from 1950–1955 to 1985–1990 and then declined by eight-tenths of a year, viz., from 29.8 years in 1985–1990 to 29.0 years in 2015–2020.

Besides the female average age of childbearing in nations at different income levels, Figure 5.2 shows the female average age of childbearing for the world as a whole. Importantly, the figure reveals that policy concerned with the female average age of childbearing should not rely on the global average and its course over time. Sharp differences exist between the three national income categories in their female average ages of childbearing, and these differences render the global average misleading. Indeed, across the periods covered by the figure, the coefficient for the correlation between the female mean age of childbearing in high-income nations and the female mean age of childbearing in middle-income nations was negative $(r = -0.44)$.[13]

The relative income level of nations, however, is relevant to more than just the female mean age of childbearing. Consideration must also be given to the total and age-specific fertility rates of the countries at each income level. As seen in section 5.3, these rates add to the demographic portrait of the global human population and offer insights into the demographic sources of change in its numerical size.

5.3 Total and age-specific fertility rates: Nations by income level

Utilizing data from the United Nations,[14] section 5.3 follows two paths. First, the TFR is compared across national income categories of countries in order to show the relative levels of childbearing within each category and movements in these

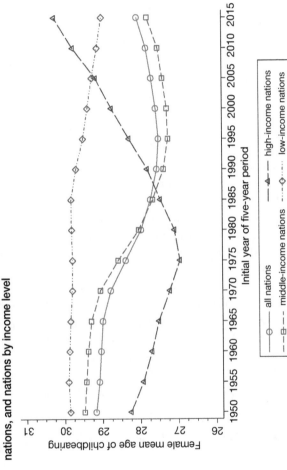

Figure 5.2: Mean childbearing age among females since the mid-twentieth century: all nations, and nations by income level

Source: See note 8 in this chapter.

levels since the middle of the twentieth century.[15] To do so, we will use Figure 5.3, but readers should keep in mind that, while higher-income nations have TFRs that are below the TFRs of lower-income nations, higher-income nations are responsible for greater harm to the biosphere.[16] The latter point is made more important by the changes that have happened over time in the number of nations in each income category. Between fiscal year 1989–1990 and fiscal year 2021–2022, for example, the number of high-income nations nearly doubled from 41 to 79, the number of middle-income nations rose from 73 to 110, and the number of low-income nations fell from 49 to 27.[17] Otherwise said, nations occupying the top rung of the income ladder, like nations comprising the middle rung, are a large, and have been a secularly growing, share of all nations. Nations in the bottom rung, on the other hand, comprise a share that is small and has been shrinking.

The second path augments the first. Specifically, on the second path, we look at high-income nations and at middle-income nations, and within each of these national income categories, we compare shares of the TFR due to different age-specific fertility rates. The comparison, which will be done using Figure 5.4, offers an opportunity to identify the age ranges of females at which birth-curtailing social and economic pressures and incentives may yield relatively large reductions in overall fertility. Females aged 45–49 are omitted from the comparison because, as seen in Table 5.1, they produce a very small percentage of births globally. Our focus is thus on the ages of females where virtually all childbearing takes place.

Turning to Figure 5.3, we see that, during the past 50 years, a large gap opened between the TFR of low-income nations and the TFR of nations where incomes are higher. The foregoing trend was accompanied by a significant narrowing of the gap between the TFR of middle-income nations and the TFR of high-income nations. The result of the narrowing is that, at the end of the 50-year period, that is, in 2015–2020, the TFR of middle-income nations (2,347 births per 1,000

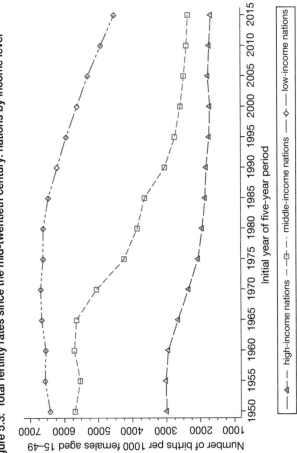

Figure 5.3: Total fertility rates since the mid-twentieth century: nations by income level

Source: See note 14 in this chapter.

women) was closer to the TFR of high-income nations (1,674 births per 1,000 women) than to the TFR of low-income nations (4,520 births per 1,000 women). However, although the poorest set of nations has had and still has a far higher TFR than the richer sets of nations, Figure 5.3 shows that the fertility of the poorest set has steadily and noticeably declined since 1980–1985. Additionally, nations in the poorest set have become fewer in number, and today the set is composed of just one out of eight nations in the world. By contrast, the TFR of middle-income nations and the TFR of high-income nations have changed little during the twenty-first century, and the number of such nations has significantly grown. Since middle- and high-income nations inflict greater damage on the biosphere than low-income nations, they warrant close attention when looking at policy measures that can safeguard the biosphere, including measures that hold promise for reducing human fertility.

The preceding discussion brings us to Figure 5.4, which presents a measure that I calculated from the total fertility rate and age-specific fertility rates. To begin with the obvious, Figure 5.4 focuses on two sets of nations—high-income nations (in the top graph) and middle-income nations (in the bottom graph)—and covers the previously used 14 five-year time intervals from 1950–1955 to 2015–2020. Low-income nations are excluded from the figure because, as discussed earlier, (1) they place comparatively little pressure on the biosphere, (2) they now comprise only about one out of eight nations in the world,[18] and (3) their TFRs are declining. In the foregoing respects, high- and middle-income nations differ markedly from low-income nations.

The central concern of the graphs in Figure 5.4 is with the relative contribution that each age-specific fertility rate made to the TFR. Specifically, for each of the 14 five-year intervals, the graphs report the *percentages*—the relative shares—of the TFR that were due to the several age-specific fertility rates other than the age-specific fertility rate of the oldest age, that is, age 45–49. The oldest age is left out because, as seen in Table 5.1, its contribution to the TFR has been very small. Nevertheless, the contribution of the oldest age to the TFR is more than zero, and a reader may thus wish to keep in mind that the sum of the percentages graphed in Figure 5.4 for a given time period is below 100.0.

An illustration may aid in understanding Figure 5.4. To return briefly to Figure 5.3, the TFR in high-income nations during 1950–1955 was 2,987 live births per 1,000 females. Of these births, Figure 5.4 shows that 29.6 percent came from females aged 25–29, and 27.4 percent came from females aged 20–24. Women aged 40–44 produced the smallest percentage (3.9 percent). Females aged 15–44 accounted for 99.6 percent of the TFR in high-income nations during 1950–1955; women aged 45–49, who are not included in the graph, were the source of just 0.4 percent.

What practical information can the graphs in Figure 5.4 supply? The percentages of a TFR arising from its component age-specific fertility rates are a potentially useful tool for identifying the ages of females at which overall childbearing might be materially reduced by policy-alterable pressures and incentives. An aid to doing so is an additional statistic, namely, the coefficient of variation. To obtain the coefficient of variation for a given set of nations, the standard deviation of the percentages for that set of nations was divided by the mean of the percentages. Two coefficients of variation are computed here—one for high-income nations and the other for middle-income nations—because the coefficients supply equivalent measures of the variability of the percentages across the two sets of nations. They do so by removing differences between the means of the percentages for the respective sets of nations and hence mean-standardize the amounts of dispersion in the percentages for the two nation-sets. Since the coefficients employ the same measurement unit (viz., percentages) and are unaffected by the magnitudes of the units in the sets,[19] the coefficients reveal whether one set of nations experienced greater variability in the percentages than the other set. The coefficients of variation for the sets of nations in Figure 5.4 are:

High-income nations	0.24
Middle-income nations	0.35

Looking at these coefficients, a tempting conclusion is that further consideration of variability in the percentages between the two sets of nations is unnecessary. As is obvious, the two coefficients are not markedly dissimilar in their numerical values. However, when these coefficients of variation are placed next to the coefficient of variation for low-income nations (namely, 0.12), we find that the coefficient for high-income nations is twice as large, and the coefficient for middle-income nations is nearly three times as large, as the coefficient for low-income nations. The percentages were thus much more volatile in the two sets of wealthier nations than in the set of poor nations, suggesting that the responsiveness of fertility to policy-changeable pressures and incentives is potentially far greater in the former two sets than in the latter set. The coefficients of variation thus give impetus to the inquiries we are undertaking here into the age-specific fertility shares of the TFR in high-income nations and in middle-income nations.

My examination of Figure 5.4 starts by considering how the figure informs the average childbearing age among females. As explained in section 5.2 *supra*, the average age is an important variable affecting whether and how quickly human-population growth comes to an end. In high-income nations, we learn from Figure 5.2, the average age for childbearing among females, after a rapid multi-decade increase, was in the 30–34 age range during the most recent period (2015–2020): To be exact, the female mean childbearing age in this period was 30.2 years.[20] The increase occurred, and occurred when it did, mainly because fertility rates at age 30–34 and at age 35–39 were becoming larger shares of the TFR, as the top graph in Figure 5.4 demonstrates. Since the growth in these shares gives

Figure 5.4: Shares of total fertility rates due to component age-specific fertility rates since the mid-twentieth century: high-income nations and middle-income nations

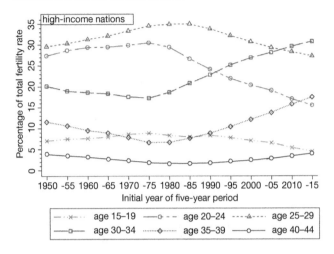

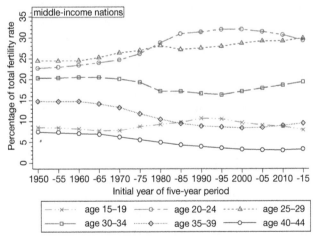

Source: Author's calculations from data in the source cited in note 14 in this chapter.

no indication of slowing down, the female mean childbearing age in high-income nations seems likely to push farther into the 30–34 age range, especially if policy is able to be supportive.

In middle-income nations, by contrast, the female mean childbearing age substantially declined during much of last half of the twentieth century (Figure 5.2), and although it then began to rise, the magnitude of the rise was small.[21] On the other hand, the bottom graph in Figure 5.4 reveals that the age 30–34 share of the TFR in middle-income nations has steadily moved upward during the last 20 years (from 16.3 percent in 1995–2000 to 19.4 percent in 2015–2020), a trend that appears capable of continuing if, inter alia, policy is kept from hindering it.

However, we are not at the end of what Figure 5.4 can tell us. In terms of high-income nations (top graph), we find that, during the latest period (2015–2020), fertility at age 20–24 and at age 35–39 contributed materially and about equally to the TFR, but that for several decades the contribution of age 20–24 has been getting smaller while the contribution of age 35–39 has been getting larger. These two ages merit attention because in combination their fertility accounted for fully one-third of the TFR in 2015–2020. The goal of stabilizing (or shrinking) the numerical size of the global human population will be facilitated insofar as policy in high-income nations is able to encourage continuation of the decreasing contribution to the TFR by women age 20–24 and, assuming that (maternal and child) health considerations do not exist, is able to avoid discouraging the increasing contribution by women age 35–39.

I turn now to middle-income nations (bottom graph) and focus on fertility at two ages, namely, age 20–24 and age 25–29. These ages merit attention because their fertility rates in combination accounted for 59.2 percent, that is, six-tenths, of the TFR in middle-income countries during the latest period (2015–2020). Moreover, the bottom graph informs us, the shares of the TFR produced by age 20–24 and age 25–29 in middle-income nations have been changing, and the changes have been substantial: Between their maximums and minimums across the 14 five-year periods, fertility rates, as shares of the TFR, moved by more than 9 percentage points at age 20–24 and by more than 5 percentage points at age 25–29. That fertility rates at these ages have been relatively elastic in the past may indicate they are able to change substantially in the future. In middle-income nations, policy can slow down population growth if it is able to shift childbearing at age 20–24 to childbearing at age 25–29 and shift childbearing at age 25–29 to childbearing at age 30–34. The presently decreasing share of the TFR due to fertility at age 15–19 (assuming that the decrease continues) will also assist in halting population growth in middle-income nations, but the effect will not be large given the insubstantial influence that childbearing at this age has on the TFR. To be precise, the share of the TFR in middle-income nations that was due to fertility at age 15–19 was just 7.9 percent during 2015–2020.

In sum, the biosphere is harmed more by the human inhabitants of high-income nations and of middle-income nations than by the human inhabitants of low-income nations. Additions to the number of people in high-income nations and middle-income nations, therefore, should be a source of concern to environmentalists. The demographic aspects of these nations that have been reviewed here suggest that age-targeted policy may be able to help in reducing human procreation in both sets of nations. This possibility warrants exploration in environmental scholarship.

5.4 Childlessness

The TFR and age-specific fertility rates are not the only measures of human reproduction that should be looked at when seeking to understand the demographic aspects of fertility. Along with the TFR and its components, the extent of childlessness merits consideration. However, when focusing on childlessness and its prevalence, two questions must be answered. First, should childlessness be studied in one sex or in both sexes? Second, if just one sex is selected for studying childlessness, should that sex be females or males?

5.4.1 Sex differences in childlessness

I answer the preceding questions by limiting myself to childlessness among females. A concentration on females is generally preferable, I believe, to a concentration on males when formulating and evaluating policy that may create incentives for childlessness. In this context, females are a better choice than males for a number of reasons:

1. Females are, of course, the only sex that conceives and gives birth to children. The number of births in a population is, in turn, a determinant of whether, and by how much, the numerical size of the population grows or declines.
2. Given the differences between females and males in the biological role that each sex plays in the reproductive process, childlessness among women is more easily and accurately measured than childlessness among men.[22] Partly as a consequence, a much larger volume of data exists on the reproductive histories of females than on the reproductive histories of males.[23] Empirically based policies that promote childlessness may thus be more easily devised for females than for males.
3. Females are biologically capable of conceiving and bearing children in a narrower range of chronological ages than males are biologically capable of fathering children.[24] As a result, policy incentives for voluntary childlessness may be simpler to design for women than for men.
4. Because females experience lower mortality rates than males,[25] females have a higher probability of surviving to the age at which their physical ability to procreate ends than males have of surviving to the age at which men can no longer procreate. Incentives for voluntary childlessness,

consequently, may be more effective as an instrument among all females than among all males.

5. The sociological conditions that lead human females to remain childless may differ from the sociological conditions that lead human males to remain childless.[26] If so, sex-dissimilar policy incentives to promote voluntary childlessness may be necessary. The above reasons recommend the formulation of incentives for females.

5.4.2 Involuntary childlessness and voluntary childlessness

Biological sex, however, is not the only basis on which to differentiate childlessness. An additional basis for differentiation is whether childlessness is involuntary or voluntary, that is, whether childlessness is the result of factors that impair the physical ability of humans to reproduce or the result of sociological, economic, and/or psychological influences that lead individuals to decide not to have children. As to involuntary childlessness, about one out of 50 women worldwide in the early twenty-first century was estimated to be physically unable to bear any children, while another five out of 50 women worldwide were estimated to have become physically unable to bear a child after having one or more births.[27] The overwhelming majority of females are physically capable of bearing children, therefore, making voluntary childlessness a promising route to lower human fertility.

The promise of voluntary childlessness is buttressed by at least two aspects of childlessness. First, childlessness among women who are too old for childbearing (that is, lifelong childlessness) has been shown to vary a great deal over time within a nation as well as between nations,[28] and since voluntary childlessness is the chief source of all childlessness, voluntary childlessness almost certainly experiences substantial variation both temporally and geographically. The magnitude of the variation indicates that voluntary lifetime childlessness may be made more common by devising and implementing incentives for childlessness among individuals who are able to procreate but have not yet done so.

A second aspect of childlessness increases the promise of voluntary childlessness as a means to combat population growth. Specifically, the susceptibility of persons who have not reproduced to incentives that encourage childlessness may be much greater than the susceptibility of persons who have already reproduced to incentives aimed at discouraging further childbearing. The dissimilarity is due to social-psychological differences associated with demographic parities, that is, the number of live births for which an individual is responsible at a particular point in time. Among female members of the human species, the social and psychological distance from zero parity (that is, no births) to parity one (first birth) may be much longer than the distance from parity one to parity two (second birth), and the distance may not appreciably change after parity two.[29] In other words, the procreative step by women from childlessness to a first child may be much harder to take, and may require considerably more social and psychological resources to take, than the step from a first child to a second child. If that is the case, antifertility incentives may accomplish more by discouraging a female from becoming a mother than by deterring a female who is already a mother from undertaking further procreation.

But will such an approach work, and if so, how well? Unfortunately, the question has yet to be answered by empirical research, and may not be answerable for quite a while. A rigorous assessment of the approach requires all of the elements of the optimal research design for gauging the effectiveness of law and policy.[30] In this regard, data for the assessment must be available for at least one nation that has law/policy encouraging childlessness (the treatment jurisdiction) and for at least one nation that does not (the control jurisdiction). Inasmuch as no nation seems to have adopted law/policy intended to promote childlessness, social scientists today are able to employ just computer modelling and simulate fertility responses to such law/policy. A real-world empirical evaluation of the ability of a law/policy provision designed to alter the incidence of childlessness cannot, therefore, be expected in the near future.

Nevertheless, let us assume that voluntary childlessness can be materially increased by law and government policy. To do so, on what should this law/policy concentrate? The findings of one study suggest that such law/policy will be most successful with types of childless, childbearing-capable adults who have a weak personal commitment to becoming parents: These adults become more likely to remain childless as the economic, social, and/or psychological costs of being a parent mount.[31] Notably, at least in economically advanced societies, the shares of such adults in the population appear to have generally expanded.[32] However, identification of the types of childless adults who are able to procreate but lack a strong interest in doing so will be just a first step, and perhaps the easiest. Next, policy/law will need to incorporate substantive provisions that promise to be effective in boosting voluntary childlessness. However, since there may be different types of childless, childbearing-capable adults, the provisions may have to vary between the types.

How should these provisions be formulated, and what should they say? To begin, lawmakers and policymakers must recognize that they will need to draw on an array of disciplines, including demography and ethics, and that these disciplines will help not only by supplying empirical research but also theory.[33] As to theory, I look at one that I believe should not be dismissed simply because of its assumption that evolution offers support for more childlessness among human beings. *Homo sapiens* belongs to the animal kingdom, after all, and the thesis that Darwinian principles apply to it is thus not unreasonable. The theory, in short, warrants attention.

5.4.3 The Aarssen-Altman theory

The central thesis of the theory (the 'Aarssen-Altman theory') is that humans have an innate drive to leave their mark on the future and that this legacy drive is satisfied by procreation, which transmits the genes of the parents to succeeding generations, *and/or* by non-procreative activities that have a lasting influence.[34] The latter activities cover a wide range and include, inter alia, the achievement of positions in government or business that carry power, personal engagement in civic organizations, and philanthropy. According to the theory, the legacy drive has been built into *Homo sapiens* by natural selection because, for all but a small fraction of the time that the human species has inhabited Earth, human individuals acted on the drive by procreating, thereby increasing the prevalence of individuals in whom the drive is strong. However, the theory points out, macro-level societal forces are now affecting how the legacy drive is manifested. To be exact, changes in social life are allowing the legacy drive to be met without engaging in reproduction. These changes, the theory emphasizes, occur in affluent, technologically advanced societies, where women have a larger number and wider range of non-procreative opportunities to fulfill their legacy drive.

Notably, an indication of the sociological significance of the growth of non-childbearing opportunities for women in a society can be found in the law that exists in the society. Law is a window that reveals dominant social ideals and practices.[35] Accordingly, scholars can learn a great deal about the place of women in a society by looking at what the law of the society says about women. This point can be illustrated using law in the United States. Being an economically advanced nation, the United States is within the scope of the Aarssen-Altman theory, and from the late nineteenth century to the end of the twentieth century, U.S. labor force participation rates—a non-procreative activity that could satisfy the legacy drive—rose steadily among married women.[36] Concomitantly, the share of U.S. women who worked in an unpaid capacity in a 'family enterprise' declined secularly from the middle of the nineteenth century onward.[37]

Labor force involvement thus evidences enlarging social opportunities for American women over more than a century, and this change had become so significant by the 1970s that it was recognized by the U.S. Supreme Court in construing the national Constitution: 'No longer,' said the Court in an opinion written in 1975, 'is the female destined solely for the home and the rearing of the family, and only the male for the marketplace and the world of ideas. Women's activities and responsibilities are increasing and expanding.'[38] As a result, the Court ruled, the equal protection guarantee of the Constitution, which prohibits government action that favors one group over another group unless a sufficient justification exists for the dissimilar treatment,[39] is violated by government action that places females at a disadvantage relative to males in terms of access to the parental financial support that is beneficial to, if not required for, schooling after age 18.[40] More generally, the Court has explained that

> neither federal nor state government acts compatibly with the equal protection principle when a law or official policy denies to women, simply because they are women, full citizenship stature—equal opportunity to aspire, achieve, participate in and contribute to society based on their individual talents and capacities.[41]

In short, the 1970s witnessed the emergence under the U.S. Constitution of judicial resistance to government actions that back social inequality for American females.[42] By this time, however, the role of women in American social life had already undergone substantial, long-term change, and the embrace of this change by constitutional law demonstrates that the change was not just societally salient but societally endorsed as well. That the change was acknowledged by constitutional law in the United States aligns with the thesis of the Aarssen–Altman theory that human beings—in the present case, American women—possess an inborn legacy drive whose satisfaction in modern nations is being redirected by macro-level social forces toward non-childrearing activities.[43]

We now reach the question of how law and government policy may be able to increase the extent of childlessness in economically advanced countries. Specifically, can social science research, in conjunction with the Aarssen-Altman theory, make any suggestions for such law/policy? The theory, of course, implies that the legacy drive, being embedded deeply in *Homo sapiens*, does not diminish, let alone disappear, as social conditions change. The theory further implies that the manifestations of the drive, while varying in form across societies of different types, are always present in some form. In an economically advanced society, where the theory anticipates that the drive will often be fulfilled by non-procreative activities, a notable study found that, among both women and men, the endorsement of female-male equality, and hence of opportunities for women that match the opportunities for men, became more prevalent as the level of formal education went up among the job-market entrants in the society, and that increases in educational attainment added to sex-role egalitarianism even when holding constant the rate at which females in the society participated in the labor force.[44] Moreover, expanding education was found to have had a larger impact on the endorsement of female-male equality by women than by men. Since the spread of schooling is more important for promoting women's sex-role egalitarianism than for promoting men's sex-role egalitarianism, schooling for females can lead women to engage in non-procreative activities rather than childbearing.

In this regard, we should not lose sight of the larger context for law/policy that supports formal schooling in a society. Such law/policy must fit comfortably within its societal context and, because of this context, can facilitate ongoing social change but cannot appreciably compel social change. Thus, the spread of education does not occur by itself in a society. Rather, the spread is part of broad sociological change, viz., societal modernization, a probable correlate if not consequence of improvements in the stock of knowledge that the society employs.[45] Importantly, this broad sociological change may have the potential to promote childlessness by increasing gender egalitarianism[46] apart from years of formal schooling.[47] In light of the foregoing possibility, a recently published multi-country study is informative: Using cross-sectional data, the researchers found that greater favorability toward sex-role equality accompanied societal modernization in a nation where less than half of the population self-identified as Muslim.[48] Of course, the progress of modernization in a society (or at least a non-Muslim society) brings more women into positions that traditionally they have not occupied, including positions in local legislative bodies that are filled by elections.[49] Accordingly, women in a modern society continue to satisfy their legacy drive, and they are able to do so through non-procreative types of activities that are open to them because of egalitarianism in sex roles. Policy incentives that support such egalitarianism among females in a society may, in turn, increase childlessness if and to the degree that the incentives are compatible with the culture and structure of the society. Unsurprisingly, overall fertility rates go down as the legacy drive is fulfilled by advances in egalitarianism among females and the convergence of the societal role of women with the societal role of men.[50]

SIX

Concluding Remarks

Human beings do not easily let go of their paradigms, and scholars are no exception. A paradigm serves to make sense of the world, or at least a segment of it, and when a paradigm is challenged, its holders react defensively. Not surprisingly, this defensiveness on the part of the individual has corollaries in groups of individuals. One such group-level corollary is inertia: Just as defensiveness characterizes an individual, social inertia characterizes a group. For a paradigm that is currently out of the mainstream, both individual defensiveness and group inertia act as obstacles that impede acceptance of the paradigm, and may completely defeat it. Individual defensiveness and group inertia can do so by creating self-reinforcing cycles that ward off novel paradigms that have begun to attract attention.[1] Paradigms change slowly, therefore, and only after they have overcome not-inconsiderable resistance.

Individual defensiveness and social inertia are relevant to the topic of the instant book, because as is obvious in the preceding chapters, the book questions the utility of any paradigm, in scholarship or elsewhere, that denies the serious and negative effects on the biosphere emanating from the present numerical size and continued numerical growth of the human population. Importantly, this paradigm is dominant today in environmental studies, an undertaking that is essentially a subject-matter focus rather than a separate academic discipline. Many disciplines share an interest in environmental studies and hence employ a paradigm that lacks a concern with human-population size and growth. At its core, then, the present book is about the defensiveness of a wide range of individual scholars, and the inertia of a wide range of groups of scholars, who devote themselves to studying the biosphere.

6.1 Baseball and the environmentalist's paradigm

Mother Nature always bats last, and she always bats 1,000.[2]

Robert K. Watson

Readers who are familiar with the sport of baseball will understand this quoted metaphor. Its meaning will hopefully be absorbed, too, by readers who are not familiar with the sport, because the metaphor drives home the point that the biosphere will in the end win every time that it is opposed by the human species. Humans, therefore, need to avoid conflict with the biosphere because they cannot match the power of their opponent. However, due to the growing presence of *Homo sapiens* on the planet, these conflicts are more common today than in the past. The increase in the conflicts is indicated by the increasing frequency of disasters: Disasters occurred more often in 2020 than in 1970, and will be even more common during the 2020s if current trends continue.[3] Still, few environmentalists acknowledge the role that the numerical increase of the human population plays in bringing about human–biosphere conflict.

Notably, environmentalists at one time recognized the damage done to the biosphere by the numerical size and increase of the human population,[4] but for some reason(s), they no longer do so. The situation will eventually change, of course, but only after environmentalists come to appreciate that their current paradigm is not working. The United Nations Environment Programme recently underscored the failure of this paradigm when it remarked that '[e]conomic, social and technological advances have come at the expense of the Earth's capacity to sustain current and future human well-being,' with the result that during the last five decades '[h]umanity's environmental challenges have grown in number and severity ... and now represent a planetary emergency.'[5]

Antarctica provides a current, and worrisome, example of the condition of the physical and biological environment of the planet. In recent decades, reductions in Antarctic ice masses have been raising the level of the oceans of the world,[6] but the Thwaites Glacier is presently attracting public attention because of its immense size—the Glacier covers approximately 74,000 square miles (192,000 square kilometers), an area that exceeds the size of the state of Florida in the United States and is almost as large as the island of Great Britain (England, Scotland, and Wales).[7] Given its mass and corresponding potential to produce higher sea levels, the Thwaites Glacier has global importance; indeed, the risks it poses have led it to be nicknamed the Doomsday Glacier. Concern has focused on the eastern ice shelf of the glacier because this shelf shows evidence of breaking off in next ten years, an event that could cause the glacier to increase by up to one-fourth what it is now adding to sea-level rise (an amount that may be as high as 4 percent of yearly increases in sea level).[8] Not surprisingly, the changes that have been occurring in and around the Thwaites Glacier are due to ice melting caused by global warming,[9] and behind this warming, of course, is the large and growing number of human beings on Earth.[10]

Another current example of the negative impact of the numerical size of the human population is the worldwide outbreak of COVID-19.[11] Notably, large-scale outbreaks of infectious disease have happened since antiquity, and they have been responsible for significant human mortality.[12] Moreover, the severity of the outbreaks in ancient times may have been due to, inter alia, the number of humans inhabiting the geographic areas where the outbreaks occurred. An illustration of an early pandemic is the Black Death during the fourteenth century—the mortality it caused is believed to have eliminated between 40 percent and 60 percent of the then-current human population of Europe, North Africa, and the Middle East.[13] Unsurprisingly, the disease persisted longer in urban areas that had a larger human population than in urban areas that had a smaller human population.[14]

Returning to the present, the ongoing spread and toll of COVID-19 has been materially facilitated by the numerical size and growth of the human population,[15] and other recent outbreaks of disease, too, can logically be assumed to have been a function of population size/growth.[16] More human beings, after all, supply more human hosts for viruses, facilitating the person-to-person transmission of viruses[17] and amplifying the potential for virus mutations.[18] Widespread outbreaks of infectious, virus-caused diseases can be expected to happen again, therefore, a prospect that is troubling even though, in the light of history, such outbreaks should not elicit surprise when they occur.

One reason that should be mentioned for expecting future health threats is the warming air temperatures involved in climate change,[19] a phenomenon that is due in part to the number of human beings and their activities.[20] Climate change has the potential to increase exposure to mosquito-carried viruses such as Zika that are harmful to human well-being.[21] Moreover, because history may be a guide to what is going to happen, we should not overlook that past changes in climate apparently contributed to the pandemics, including the Black Death pandemic, that killed large numbers of people during the period from the fourteenth century to the eighteenth century A.D.[22]

6.2 A 'proceed cautiously' sign for law and policy

The social sciences are steered by the assumption that societal change is due to society-level conditions and forces such as social divisions, culture, and advances in knowledge.[23] Under this assumption, law and government policy that targets a society-significant activity (including law/policy that authorizes and pays for family-planning programs to reduce unwanted childbearing) is considered to be the result of society-level agents and a means of satisfying a public need that these agents have created. If the assumption is correct—and social scientists have adduced considerable evidence supporting it[24]—a change in the frequency of an activity that occurs after the introduction or expansion of a program authorized by law/policy is mainly due to the large-scale forces that are responsible for bringing about the adoption of the law/policy; as a result, while the program leads to some change in activity incidence, its contribution is comparatively small.[25] The content of law/policy, in other words, is essentially a society-created bridge to a society-created end, and as such, it works with rather than against existing social-economic conditions.[26]

The case studies in section 4.3 of Chapter Four add a further dimension to a consideration of law and government policy. Specifically, the case studies erect a 'proceed cautiously' road sign for advocates of law and government policy, including advocates who want to end the numerical growth of species *Homo sapiens*. A 'proceed cautiously' approach is prudent because in response to law and policy measures, human societies can act in unexpected ways and generate outcomes that are at variance with what the advocates of the law and policy measures hoped to accomplish. Regrettably, sociologists today are largely in the dark regarding social side effects that sabotage well-intentioned law and policy.

An additional reason for caution exists with respect to efforts to combat human-population growth. Specifically, the discipline of ecology has found that the viability of an ecosystem is tied to the degree of heterogeneity in the ecosystem. Thus, an ecosystem made up of diverse components is more likely to thwart, and avoid long-term damage from, exogenic threats than an ecosystem whose components are the same or very similar.[27] The foregoing point warrants attention here because a system in the social life of human beings, and not only a system in the biosphere, may be aided by having varied components. If this is the case and social heterogeneity increases the adaptability of a societal system of *Homo sapiens*,[28] we should look carefully at how a proposed law/policy could affect the demographic structure of families in a society because diversity in completed family size may benefit a human social system just as biospheric diversity benefits an ecosystem. Putting the matter differently, the ability of a human societal system to withstand and recover from external shocks may be improved by a mixture of family sizes, and a society in which the range of family sizes is broad may have an advantage, possibly a major advantage, over a society in which the range of family sizes is narrow. When pursuing the numerical stabilization or decline of the population of *Homo sapiens*, therefore, fertility-inhibiting law/policy may need to be judged by whether a particular aggregate number of births occurred, not by whether family size was kept below a certain number of children.

How can sociological traps that generate severe, counterproductive effects be avoided? A necessary, though probably not sufficient, condition for sidestepping the traps will be to formulate law and policy measures in a setting that is multidisciplinary and interdisciplinary. The intellectual tent under which measures concerned with population growth and size are constructed will have to be very broad because the measures must build on expertise from an array of disciplines. Among these disciplines are (in alphabetical order) demography, ecology, economics, ethics, political science, psychology, religion, and sociology. Numerous disciplines are required because the excessive numerical size of the population of *Homo sapiens* is not a simple problem. Although the control of population size necessitates control over fertility, fertility has multiple dimensions, as Chapter Five pointed out.

6.3 Environmentalism's paradigm

We thus return to the paradigm that currently dominates environmentalism. Simply said, paradigm has not, despite some successes, been able to end, let alone reverse, the overall degradation of the biosphere—nor will it do so in the future.[29] The current paradigm in environmentalism is failing because it is unconcerned with how many people are on planet Earth even though, as the research covered in Chapter Two underscores, human-population size and growth are a chief source of the damage that the biosphere has been experiencing. The view that environmentalism presently has of the world inhibits, in turn, scholarly interest in devising law and government policy that may ameliorate demographic pressures on the biosphere. Environmental scholarship will thus continue to be hampered in safeguarding the biosphere and curbing the intensity of the Anthropocene until it has a paradigm that both accepts the adage 'whatever your cause, it's a lost cause without population control'[30] and begins to formulate specific suggestions for law/policy that may contribute to limiting the numerical size and growth of the human population.[31]

Eventually, of course, increases in the numerical size of the population of *Homo sapiens* will stop because these increases are altering the biosphere in ways that push up the incidence of human mortality[32] and push down the incidence of human fertility.[33] The time when human-population growth comes to an end, moreover, may not be far in the future. Indeed, the experiment that *Homo sapiens* has been conducting on the biosphere may be about to do more than halt human-population growth—it may, in Malthusian ways, appreciably reduce the number of human beings on the planet.[34] In the present context, therefore, environmentally oriented scholars can help by working to identify new law and government policies that permit *Homo sapiens* to make a humane transition to a population size that is numerically stable, or even much smaller.

Notes

one Paradigms, Environmentalism, and Demography

1   *See* Tami Moore et al., *Faculty Epistemologies and Academic Life: Implications for the Professoriate*, 7 J. PROFESSORIATE 26, 29 (2013) (describing paradigms as the expression of 'what is real to us, how we know what we know about that reality and what methods allow us to gather more information').

2   *E.g.*, Jean-Michel Claverie & Chantel Abergel, *Giant Viruses: The Difficult Breaking of Multiple Epistemological Barriers*, 59 STUD. HIST. & PHIL. BIOLOGICAL & BIOMEDICAL SCI. 89, 91, 94, 96, 98 (2016).

3   David M. Sanbonmatsu & Katie K. Sanbonmatsu, THE STRUCTURE OF SCIENTIFIC REVOLUTIONS: *Kuhn's Misconceptions of (Normal) Science*, 37 J. THEORETICAL & PHIL. PSYCHOL. 133, 149 (2017).

4   *See* Mary Jo Nye, *Kuhnian and Post-Kuhnian Views of How Science Evolves*, *in* SHIFTING PARADIGMS: THOMAS S. KUHN AND THE HISTORY OF SCIENCE 287, 291–92 (A. Blum et al. eds., 2016) (observing that studies of the history of science have found that science is dominated by 'gradualism and continuity').

5   J. Douglas Toma, *Understanding Why Scholars Choose to Work in Alternative Inquiry Paradigms*, 40 RES. HIGHER EDUC. 539, 544–45 & tbl. 2, 564 (1999).

6   Jerome McCristal Culp, Jr., *Firing Legal Canons and Shooting Blanks: Finding a Neutral Way in the Law*, 10 ST. LOUIS U. PUB. L. REV. 185, 186 (1991).

7   Iván González-Márquez & Victor M. Toledo, *Sustainability Science: A Paradigm in Crisis?*, 12(7) SUSTAINABILITY art. 2802, at 1, 10–11, 13–14 (2020). Sustainability science is defined as the study of interventions that can develop and maintain an environment for *Homo sapiens* that supplies not just the necessities of human survival but also economic security and social equity. William C. Clark & Alicia G. Harley, *Sustainability Science: Toward a Synthesis*, 45 ANN. REV. ENV'T & RESOURCES 331, 333, 336 tbl. 1 (2020). Consequently, sustainability science is transdisciplinary, that is, involves more than one field of scholarship. David J. Rapport, *Sustainability Science: An Ecohealth Perspective*, 2 SUSTAINABILITY SCI. 77 (2007).

8   Nicholas A. Robinson, *Legal Systems, Decisionmaking, and the Science of Earth's Systems: Procedural Missing Links*, 27 ECOLOGY L. Q. 1077, 1161 (2001).

9   LARRY D. BARNETT, DEMOGRAPHY AND THE ANTHROPOCENE 3–4 (2021) [hereinafter DEMOGRAPHY AND THE ANTHROPOCENE]. 'Wild law' and environmental law share the tenet that the biosphere hosts the human

species and is the context in which *Homo sapiens* exists, but the two fields are distinguishable. The elements of wild law are described in CORMAC CULLINAN, WILD LAW: A MANIFESTO FOR EARTH JUSTICE 30–31, 44–48, 60, 90–91, 160, 170 (2d ed, 2011). A key distinction between wild law and environmental law is that the former is more jurisprudential than the latter—in particular, wild law posits that the biosphere possesses inherent, legally cognizable rights. Glen Wright, *Climate Regulation as if the Planet Mattered: The Earth Jurisprudence Approach to Climate Change*, 3 BARRY U. ENVTL. & EARTH LAW J. 33, 43–45, 48 (2013). This postulate has traditionally not been accepted by environmental law. Susana Borràs, *New Transitions from Human Rights to the Environment to the Rights of Nature*, 5 TRANSNAT'L ENVTL. L. 113 (2016). Nonetheless, wild law is like environmental law in lacking interest in the negative biospheric consequences of the number of human beings on Earth. *See* CULLINAN, *supra*, a book of approximately 200 text pages; the index in the book contains an entry for 'population' that references just four pages mentioning human-population size/growth. *See also* MICHELLE MALONEY & PETER BURDON (EDS.), WILD LAW—IN PRACTICE (2014), a book consisting of 16 separately authored chapters that together cover approximately 260 text pages; the index in the book has a single entry pertinent to human demography, viz., an entry for 'population growth,' and this entry references just one page.

[10] *See* Haydn Washington et al., *Why Do Society and Academia Ignore the 'Scientists Warning to Humanity' on Population?*, 25 J. FUTURES STUD. 93, 94, 102 (2020) (contending that Earth will be unable over the long run to provide adequately for *Homo sapiens* because of (1) human-population increase and consumption of resources and (2) growth-oriented economies; observing that 'the public, governments and much of academia have been shying away from these issues for decades' and that 'society is in denial of all of them'). *See also* Karin Kuhlemann, *Complexity, Creeping Normalcy and Conceit: Sexy and Unsexy Risks*, 21 FORESIGHT 35, 36–37 (2019) (discussing aspects of cognition that reduce the ability of human beings to acknowledge and effectively respond to overpopulation as a 'global catastrophic risk').

[11] INTERGOVERNMENTAL SCIENCE-POLICY PLATFORM ON BIODIVERSITY AND ECOSYSTEM SERVICES, THE GLOBAL ASSESSMENT REPORT ON BIODIVERSITY AND ECOSYSTEM SERVICES: SUMMARY FOR POLICYMAKERS 37 (2019).

[12] William J. Ripple et al., *World Scientists' Warning to Humanity: A Second Notice*, 67 BIOSCIENCE 1026, 1026 (2017).

[13] Johannes Lohwasser et al., *The Role of Demographic and Economic Drivers on the Environment and Standardized STIRPAT Analysis*, 178 ECOLOGICAL ECON. art. 106811, at 6 (2020).

[14] Yoonjung Yi & Amaël Borzée, *Human Population and Efficient Conservation: Are Humans Playing Ostriches and Rabbits?*, 14 J. ASIA-PACIFIC BIODIVERSITY 144, 144 (2021) (contending that 'a widespread taboo' applies at the present time to discourse regarding government efforts to control population size).

[15] Joseph A. Tainter, *Archaeology of Overshoot and Collapse*, 35 ANN. REV. ANTHROPOLOGY 59, 71–72 (2006).

[16] Mauricio Lima, *Climate Change and the Population Collapse During the 'Great Famine' in Pre-Industrial Europe*, 4 ECOLOGY & EVOLUTION 284, 287 (2014), https://doi.org/10.1002/ece3.936.

[17] Christopher Bystroff, *Footprints to Singularity: A Global Population Model Explains Late 20th Century Slow-Down and Predicts Peak within Ten Years*, 16(5) PLoS ONE art. e0247214, at 1, 6, 9 (2021) (using long-term data in a model concerned with the capacity of the biosphere to support the human species; concluding that the number of human beings on the planet may be reaching its maximum and may soon start to decrease sharply).

[18] Stata® IC version 12.1 was used to construct the graphs, and carry out the statistical analyses, in the instant book.

[19] Global Footprint Network, https://data.footprintnetwork.org/#/about theData (definition of 'ecological footprint'). The Global Footprint Network currently provides estimates of the ecological footprint of *Homo sapiens* for each year, starting with 1961 and ending with 2018. Global Footprint Network, Analyze by Land Types, https://data.footprintnetw ork.org/#/analyzeTrends?type=earth&cn=5001 (under 'Select Country or Region,' choose 'World'; under 'Select Type,' choose 'Ecological Footprint (Number of Earths)'; click on 'Download Data') (last visited July 23, 2022).

[20] Numerous impediments exist in determining the threshold. For a summary of the impediments, see J. Kenneth Small, *Beyond Population Stabilization: The Case for Dramatically Reducing Global Human Numbers*, 16 POL. & LIFE SCI. 183, 187 (1997).

[21] GLOBAL FOOTPRINT NETWORK, ECOLOGICAL FOOTPRINT ACCOUNTING 10 (2020), https://www.footprintnetwork.org/our-work/ecological-footpr int/limitations-and-criticisms. The ecological footprint encompasses 'all the mutually exclusive, biologically productive spaces that human activity demands.' Mutually exclusive spaces prevent the same space from being counted more than once. *Id.* at 10 n.10. The ecological footprint measure is not without limitations; see *id.* at 29–38 for a review and discussion of criticisms of the measure.

[22] Theodore P. Lianos & Anastasia Pseiridis, *Sustainable Welfare and Optimum Population Size*, 18 ENVTL DEV. & SUSTAINABILITY 1679, 1688, 1689 tbl. 1, 1695 (2016) (using the amount of cultivated land to compute the

numerical size of the global population that can be supplied indefinitely with the current economic level of the average resident of Europe; finding that, in 2010, this 'desired' number was less than half the number of human beings believed to inhabit the planet).

23 Fiorenzo Facchini, *Man, Origin and Nature, in* INTERDISCIPLINARY ENCYCLOPEDIA OF RELIGION AND SCIENCE (G. Tanzella-Nitti et al. eds., 2002), http://inters.org/origin-nature-of-man (last visited May 2, 2021).

24 Nelson J. R. Fagundes et al., *Statistical Evaluation of Alternative Models of Human Evolution*, 104(45) PROC. NAT'L ACAD. SCI. 17614, 17615 tbl. 1 (2007).

25 The evidence that these and other problems are generated by overpopulation is cited in DEMOGRAPHY AND THE ANTHROPOCENE, *supra* note 9, at 19–31. In addition, see Monica H. Green, *The Four Black Deaths*, 125 AM. HIST. REV. 1601 (2020) for a historiographic study of the Black Death pandemic and its impact on human societies. The Black Death, which is thought to have been caused by a bacterium, may be the single worst pandemic ever experienced by *Homo sapiens* and was increased by areas of human-population concentration. Green, *supra*, at 1601, 1603, 1607, 1627. Professor Green advances the thesis that the Black Death pandemic 'was even larger than previously imagined,' having begun a century earlier and been far more geographically widespread than commonly assumed. Green, *supra*, at 1602, 1607, 1615, 1625, 1627.

26 For the design and findings of the study on which this conclusion is based, see DEMOGRAPHY AND THE ANTHROPOCENE, *supra* note 9, at 35–50.

27 *Id.* at 10, 11–13 & fig. 1.3.

28 *Id.* at 3. *Accord*, Haydn Washington et al., *supra* note 10, at 94.

29 Scott Fulton & Nicholas A. Robinson, *Foreword, in* MARIA ANTONIA TIGRE, GAPS IN INTERNATIONAL ENVIRONMENTAL LAW: TOWARD A GLOBAL PACT FOR THE ENVIRONMENT xiii, xix (2019) (observing in November 2019 that '[f]ifty years ago' environmental law was not an established, recognized discipline). *See* Elisabeth Fisher et al., *Maturity and Methodology: Starting a Debate about Environmental Law Scholarship*, 21 J. ENVTL. L. 213 (2009) (accepting and critiquing the position taken by environmental-law scholars that scholarship in environmental law has yet to mature).

30 Irfan Khan et al., *The Impact of Natural Resources, Energy Consumption, and Population Growth on Environmental Quality: Fresh Evidence from the United States of America*, 764 SCI. TOTAL ENV'T art. 142222, at 1, 5, 7 (2021) (analyzing data on the United States for the years 1971 through 2016); Xiaotian Yang & Irfan Khan, *Dynamics among Economic Growth, Urbanization, and Environmental Sustainability in IEA Countries: The Role of Industry Value-Added*, 29 ENVTL. SCI & POLLUTION RES. 4116, 4119, 4123 & tbl. 7 (2022) (studying the 30 nations that were members of the

International Energy Agency; analyzing data on these nations for the years 1992 through 2016).

[31] Adam Vaughan, *Birthplace of the Anthropocene*, 250(3333) NewScientist, May 8, 2021, at 12.

[32] Simon L. Lewis & Mark A. Maslin, *Defining the Anthropocene*, 519 Nature, March 12, 2015, at 171; Richard Monastersky, *The Human Age*, 519 Nature, March 12, 2015, at 144.

[33] For estimates of the size of the global human population since 10,000 BC, see: U.S. Census Bureau, Historical Estimates of World Population (2021), https://www.census.gov/data/tables/time-series/demo/intern ational-programs/historical-est-worldpop.html; Max Roser et al., Our World in Data, World Population Growth (2019), https://ourworldind ata.org/world-population-growth.

[34] Figure 1.2 is based on the median-variant estimates of mid-year world population size in the 'WPP2019_TotalPopulationBySex.csv' Excel file of the U.N. Dep't of Econ. & Soc. Affairs, Population Div., *Population Dynamics* (online ed.), https://population.un.org/wpp/Download/Stand ard/Population (on this page, select 'CSV format,' and for subgroup 'Total Population,' click on 'All variants' file) (last visited June 20, 2021). I used these U.N.-published estimates to calculate the midyear-to-midyear numerical and percent changes that are graphed in Figure 1.2. The Excel file provides estimates of mid-year population size for all years through mid-2020; the estimates are from data gathered in censuses and surveys. The data on population size for all years through 2020 are not projections. U.N. Dep't of Econ. & Soc. Affairs, Population Div., World Population Prospects 2019: Methodology of the United Nations Population Estimates and Projections [hereinafter U.N. Methodology], https://population.un.org/wpp/Methodology. Estima tes of global population size since 1920 are in Demography and the Anthropocene, *supra* note 9, at 7–10 & fig. 1.1.

[35] Across the entire period covered by the figure, the two variables (numerical increase and growth rate) were negatively correlated (r = -0.45). Approximately one-fifth of the variation in one variable could thus be explained by variation in the other variable (r^2 = -0.45 x -0.45 = .203 x 100 = 20.3 percent). The correlation coefficient (that is, r) was based on 70 observations. r, which was computed using the CORRELATE command in Stata® IC 12.1, is the Pearson product-moment correlation coefficient. StataCorp, Stata Base Reference Manual Release 12, at 393–400, 2371 (2011).

[36] Figure 1.3 uses the estimates of the global total fertility rate in the 'WPP2019_Period_Indicators_Medium' Excel file of the U.N. Dep't of Econ. & Soc. Affairs, Population Div., *Population Dynamics* (online ed.), https://population.un.org/wpp/Download/Standard/Population

(on this page, select 'CSV format,' and for subgroup 'Period Indicators,' click on 'Medium variant (most used)' file) (last visited June 11, 2021).

[37] For a comparison of the Total Fertility Rate and the Cumulative Birth Rate with an illustration from the United States, see DEMOGRAPHY AND THE ANTHROPOCENE, *supra* note 9, at 67–71.

[38] Joseph A. McFalls, Jr., *Population: A Lively Introduction (5th ed.)*, 62(1) POPULATION BULL., March 2007, at 6 Box 2. Although the TFR is typically computed on the assumption that births occur to females who are in the age range 15 to 49, age 10 is occasionally set as the beginning of the childbearing period, and age 44 is often set as the end.

The assumption that the ability of human females to become pregnant and carry a pregnancy to term starts at age 15 and stops at age 49 generally aligns with evidence from research. A multi-country study using samples of women in eleven nations found that, for the beginning of menstruation, the tenth and ninetieth percentiles were, respectively, age 12 and age 17 (median age = 14), and that, for the end of menstruation, the tenth and ninetieth percentiles were, respectively, age 44 and age 58 (median age = 50). Alfredo Morabia et al., *International Variability in Ages at Menarche, First Live Birth, and Menopause*, 148 AM. J. EPIDEMIOLOGY 1195, 1198 tbl. 2, 1200 tbl. 3 (1998) (ranges and medians for all of the nations combined).

[39] Eurostat, *Glossary: Fertility* (italics added to quotation), https://ec.eur opa.eu/eurostat/statistics-explained/index.php?title=Glossary:Fertility.

[40] The data in Column 2 are from U.N. Population Div., Dep't of Econ. & Soc. Affairs, *World Population Prospects 2019. File FERT/7: Age-Specific Fertility Rates by Region, Subregion and Country, 1950–2100 (Births per 1,000 Women) – Estimates, 1950–2020*, https://population.un.org/wpp/ Download/Standard/Fertility (in columns 'Sub Group' and 'Files,' select respectively 'Age Composition' and 'Age-specific Fertility Rates') (last visited Dec. 9, 2021).

[41] Across this period, the two variables (numerical increase and TFR) were negatively correlated ($r = -0.77$). Approximately three-fifths of the variation in one variable could thus be explained by variation in the other variable ($r^2 = -0.77 \times -0.77 = .593 \times 100 = 59.3$ percent). The correlation coefficient (that is, r) was based on fourteen observations. Also see *supra* note 35.

[42] Replacement-level fertility is also known in demography as 'replacement fertility' and 'replacement rate fertility.'

[43] John Craig, U.K. Office of Population Censuses & Surveys, *Replacement Level Fertility and Future Population Growth*, POPULATION TRENDS, Winter 1994, at 20. Immigration and emigration are typically not considered in estimating replacement-level fertility for a nation. *Id.* at 17. The age structure of a pool of migrants in a nation, however, can affect the

number of births and deaths in the nation and hence the fertility required to replace the population of the nation. *Id.* at 21. The population of the world, of course, is not altered by migration.

[44] Steve Smallwood & Jessica Chamberlain, U.K. Office for Nat'l Stat., *Replacement Fertility, What Has It Been and What Does It Mean*, POPULATION TRENDS, Spring 2005, at 16, 16.

[45] During the period 1990–2017, the sex ratio at birth in the world as a whole is estimated to have been between 1.068 and 1.078, that is, between 106.8 and 107.8 boys per 100 girls. Fengqing Chao et al., *Systematic Assessment of the Sex Ratio at Birth for All Countries and Estimation of National Imbalances and Regional Reference Levels*, 116(19) PROC. NAT'L ACAD. SCI. 9303, 9303, 9305 tbl. 1 (corrected version June 26, 2019). *See generally* W. Dondorp et al., *ESHRE Task Force on Ethics and Law 20: Sex Selection for Non-Medical Reasons*, 28 HUM. REPROD. 1448, 1448–49 (2013) (reviewing sex-selection medical technologies); William H. James & Victor Grech, *A Review of the Established and Suspected Causes of Variations in Human Sex Ratio at Birth*, 109 EARLY HUM. DEV. 50 (2017) (reviewing stress- and hormone-caused sources of variability in the sex ratio at birth).

[46] This list is confined to demographic factors because the replacement-level fertility rate is a demographic measure. Non-demographic factors in a society, especially environmental and economic goals, can provide an impetus for a fertility rate that is less than the replacement rate for the society. Wolfgang Lutz et al., *The Future of Fertility: Future Trends in Family Size among Low Fertility Populations*, *in* WHITHER THE CHILD? CAUSES AND CONSEQUENCES OF LOW FERTILITY 205, 219, 220–21, 223 (Eric P. Kaufmann & W. Bradford Wilcox eds., 2013).

[47] Stuart Gietel-Basten & Sergei Scherbov, *Exploring the 'True Value' of Replacement Rate Fertility*, 39 POPULATION RES. & POL'Y REV. 763, 770 (2020). Calculation of replacement-level fertility is illustrated in Smallwood & Chamberlain, *supra* note 44, at 18.

[48] The global replacement-level fertility rate is estimated to have fallen from 2.96 live births per woman in 1950–1955 to 2.29 live births per woman in 2010–2015. The share of the global population for which the TFR is at or below the replacement-level fertility rate is estimated to have been 3.1 percent in 1950–1955 and 46.1 percent in 2010–2015; it is expected to peak at roughly 70 percent during the years 2020–2025 to 2050–2055. Stuart Gietel-Basten & Sergei Scherbov, *Is Half the World's Population Really Below 'Replacement-Rate'?*, 14(12) PLoS ONE art. 0224985, at 4, 6 fig. 2 (2019).

[49] U.N. DEP'T OF ECON. & SOC. AFFAIRS, POPULATION DIV., WORLD POPULATION PROSPECTS 2019. VOL. I: COMPREHENSIVE TABLES, at 2–8

tbls. A.1, A.2, & A.3 (2019), https://www.un.org/development/desa/pd/content/publications. The data are for the mid-point of each year.

A more recent edition of *World Population Prospects* contains insufficient detail to allow Figure 1.4 to be updated. U.N. Dep't of Econ. & Soc. Affairs, Population Div., World Population Prospects 2022: Summary of Results (2022). Moreover, this edition warns that the COVID-19 pandemic has resulted in 'incomplete' evidence on population trends and that the effect of the pandemic on these trends may remain unknown 'for many years.' *Id.* at 1.

[50] The three variants and their calculation are explained in U.N. Methodology, *supra* note 34.

[51] Also see Bystroff, *supra* note 17.

[52] *Supra* note 49.

[53] Recorded confirmed deaths worldwide from the COVID-19 pandemic prior to July 1, 2020 comprised 8.5 percent of all deaths attributed to COVID-19 through June 30, 2022. Computed from Our World in Data COVID-19 Dataset (owid-covid-data Excel file) available at https://ourworldindata.org/covid-deaths?country= (last visited July 24, 2022).

[54] Nazrul Islam et al., *Effects of COVID-19 Pandemic on Life Expectancy and Premature Mortality in 2020: Time Series Analysis in 37 Countries*, 375(8313) BMJ art. e066768, at 1, 2, 4 (2021) (estimating mortality caused by COVID-19 during calendar year 2020 in thirty-seven high income and upper-middle income nations; finding that COVID-19 was responsible for a substantial mortality increase in 31 nations, where the total number of years of life lost due to COVID-19 was estimated to be 17.3 million among males and 10.8 million among females), https://www.bmj.com/content/375/bmj-2021-066768. The demographic impact of the COVID-19 pandemic is more realistically measured by change in years of life lost than by change in life expectancy at birth. As a measure of the impact of the pandemic, years of life lost in a population are preferable because they are affected by both mortality in the population and the age composition of the population. On the other hand, life expectancy at birth in a population, while affected by mortality rates, is unaffected by the age composition of the population. *Id.* at 2.

[55] Arindam Nandi & Sumit Mazumdar, *The Effect of Natural Disaster on Fertility, Birth Spacing, and Child Sex Ratio: Evidence from a Major Earthquake in India*, 31 J. Population Econ. 267, 288 (2018); Valeria Scapini & Cinthya Vergara, *Natural Disasters and Birth Rate: Evidence from the 2010 Chilean Earthquake*, 29 J. Population & Soc. Stud. 274, 281, 283 (2021). *But cf.* Noriaki Kurita, *Association of the Great East Japan Earthquake and the Daiichi Nuclear Disaster in Fukushima City, Japan, With Birth Rates*, 2(1) JAMA Network Open art. e187455 (2019) (studying a city located near a nuclear plant that, due to an earthquake, released a substantial amount

of radioactive material; estimating that the release was responsible, during the next two years, for a 10 percent reduction in the birth rate in the city but that, after two years, the release did not affect the birth rate in the city), doi:10.1001/jamanetworkopen.2018.7455.

Social disruptions seem often to reduce the sex ratio at birth. Nandi & Mazumdar, *supra*, at 280, 282 tbl. 2, 290; James & Grech, *supra* note 45, at 51, 55. A changed ratio of boys to girls at birth will, in turn, affect the replacement-level fertility rate for a population. Text accompanying *supra* notes 43 to 46.

[56] U.N. Environment Programme, Global Environment Outlook (GEO-6): Summary for Policymakers 4, 19, 22 (2019) (also noting that 'population growth [is] one of the major drivers of environmental degradation') [hereinafter UNEP Summary for Policymakers], https://wedocs.unep.org/handle/20.500.11822/27652.

[57] Jayshree Pandya, *The Race to Mine Space*, Forbes, May 13, 2019, https://www.forbes.com/sites/cognitiveworld/2019/05/13/the-race-to-mine-space/?sh=3d57b4461a70. *See* Laszlo Keszthelyi et al., U.S. Geological Surv., Feasibility Study for the Quantitative Assessment of Mineral Resources in Asteroids 11 (2017) (estimating that 'the amount of useful resources in NEOs [near-Earth objects] is immense' but observing that their extraction will require major advances in technology), https://pubs.er.usgs.gov/publication/ofr20171041.

[58] Luke Thompson, Gambling News (May 5, 2021) (quote attributed to a Chinese proverb), https://www.gamblingnews.com/blog/ gambling-quotes.

two Impacts of Human Population Size and Growth: Recent Research

[1] Larry D. Barnett, Demography and the Anthropocene 19–31 (2021) [hereinafter Demography and the Anthropocene].

[2] Wayne C. Zipperer et al., *Urban Development and Environmental Degradation*, *in* Oxford Research Encyclopedia: Environmental Science 1, 17 (2020), https://doi.org/10.1093/acrefore/9780199389414.013.97.

The 'biosphere' is definable as '[t]he whole of the region of the earth's surface, the sea, and the air that is inhabited by living organisms.' Oxford Univ. Press, Oxford Reference, *Biosphere*, https://www.oxfordreference.com/view/10.1093/oi/authority.20110803095507469. At a planetary scale, the biosphere includes the ecosystem(s) of Earth. Guido Kraemer et al., *Summarizing the State of the Terrestrial Biosphere in Few Dimensions*, 17 Biogeosciences 2397, 2399, 2414 (2020). An 'ecosystem' is defined in note 15 in *infra* Chapter Four.

[3] For an explanation of the ecological-footprint measure, see notes 19 & 21 and their accompanying text in *supra* Chapter One.

[4] Samuel Asumadu Sarkodie, *Environmental Performance, Biocapacity, Carbon & Ecological Footprint of Nations: Drivers, Trends and Mitigation Options*, 751 Sci. Total Env't art. 141912, at 1, 2, 7 tbl. 1 (models 3 & 4) (2021) (finding, with other variables held constant, a 'strong effect of population density on ecological footprint'). *Accord*, Xiaotian Yang & Irfan Khan, *Dynamics among Economic Growth, Urbanization, and Environmental Sustainability in IEA Countries: The Role of Industry Value-Added*, 29 Envtl. Sci & Pollution Res. 4116, 4199, 4123 & tbl. 7 (2022) (analyzing data covering 1992–2016 on the 30 nations that were members of the International Energy Agency; holding constant, inter alia, the share of the population that resided in an urban area; finding that a 1 percentage point increase in the rate of population growth in a nation was associated with a 0.76 percent expansion of the ecological footprint of the nation). *See also* Qiang Wang et al., *Does Urbanization Redefine the Environmental Kuznets Curve? An Empirical Analysis of 134 Countries*, 76 Sustainable Cities & Soc'y art. 103382, at 1, 3–4, 12 (2022) (analyzing data on a panel of 134 nations during the period 1996–2015; finding that an increase in the urban population of a nation as a share of the total population of the nation intensified the negative impact of economic growth on the ecological footprint of the nation).

[5] See text accompanying notes 53 and 54 in *supra* Chapter One.

[6] Soeren Metelmann et al., *Impact of Climatic, Demographic and Disease Control Factors on the Transmission Dynamics of COVID-19 in Large Cities Worldwide*, 12 One Health art. 100221, at 1, 2, 3 tbl. 1 (2021).

[7] Pierre Nguimkeu & Sosson Tadadjeu, *Why Is the Number of COVID-19 Cases Lower than Expected in Sub-Saharan Africa? A Cross-Sectional Analysis of the Role of Demographic and Geographic Factors*, 138 World Dev. art. 105251, at 1, 2, 6 & tbl. 3 (2021) (analyzing data on 154 nations across the world; reporting that an increase of 1 percent in the number of people per square kilometer (the measure of population density) raised the number of COVID-19 active cases by approximately one-fourth of 1 percent; reasoning that greater population density can be expected to elevate the probability of 'inter-community contagion, even under social distancing measures'; and reporting that a gain of 1 percentage point in the fraction of the population living in an urban area increased the number of active cases by between 3.1 percent and 3.7 percent). Also see Dianna Chang et al., *The Determinants of COVID-19 Morbidity and Mortality across Countries* 1, 3, 8–10, 32–33 tbl. 2, 34–35 app. A (Nanyang Bus. School Research Paper No. 21–06, 2021) (studying a set of 109 nations and a set of 98 nations; using data on COVID-19 morbidity and mortality through the end of 2020; finding that nation-level COVID-19 morbidity

and mortality were each increased by an increment in population size as well as by an increment in the indicator of population density, that is, the share of the population located in an urban area), https://papers.ssrn.com/sol3/papers.cfm?abstract_id=3824101.

[8]   Julian Gardiner et al., *Obesity as a Driver of International Differences in COVID-19 Death Rates*, 23 DIABETES, OBESITY & METABOLISM 1463, 1464, 1466–67 & tbl. 4 (2021). The Gardiner et al. study was limited to nations that not only had the specified minimum population size and level of wealth, but also produced data whose accuracy was deemed to be acceptable. *Id.* at 1464.

   Accord, Ondrej Hradsky & Arnost Komarek, *Demographic and Public Health Characteristics Explain Large Part of Variability in COVID-19 Mortality Across Countries*, 31 EUR. J. PUB. HEALTH 12, 13, 14 tbl. 1 (2021) (studying 138 nations; using unstandardized regression coefficients; finding that, holding constant inter alia the percentage of the population that resided in an urban area, the death rate from COVID-19 rose as population density increased).

[9]   Jie Chen et al., *What Determines City's Resilience Against Epidemic Outbreak: Evidence from China's COVID-19 Experience*, 70 SUSTAINABLE CITIES & SOC'Y art. 102892, at 1, 4, 5, 7 tbl. 2 (model 5) (2021) (using data on 120 prefecture-level cities in China; finding that, holding constant population density in the urbanized area of cities, the time required to stop the spread of COVID-19 infections lengthened as city population size grew larger; also finding that, holding constant city population size, the length of time necessary to halt the spread of infections was unrelated to population density in the urbanized area of cities).

[10] Hill Kulu & Peter Dorey, *Infection Rates from Covid-19 in Great Britain by Geographical Units*, 67 HEALTH & PLACE art. 102460, at 1, 8 & tbl. 3 (2021).

[11] Devarupa Gupta et al., *COVID-19 Outbreak and Urban Dynamics: Regional Variations in India*, 86 GEOJOURNAL, at [6] tbl. 2, [14], [15] tbl. 8 (published online March 2021) (using data on 640 districts in India), https://doi.org/10.1007/s10708-021-10394-6).

[12] Onur Baser, *Population Density Index and Its Use for Distribution of COVID-19: A Case Study Using Turkish Data*, 125 HEALTH POL'Y 148, 150 (2021) (finding that, ceteris paribus, the number of COVID-19 infections in cities in Turkey was 0.67 percent higher for each 1.0 percent increase in population density, where cities were weighted by the size of their population rather than by the amount of their land space).

[13] Klaus Desmet & Romain Wacziarg, *JUE Insight: Understanding Spatial Variation in COVID-19 across the United States*, J. URB. ECON. 1, 4, 6 tbl. 2 (2021), https://doi.org/10.1016/j.jue.2021.103332 (finding that, in U.S. counties, the number of reported COVID-19 cases and the number of reported COVID-19 deaths went up, ceteris paribus, with

both 'effective local density,' that is, mean number of people per square kilometer, and with mean number of residents per household); Leon S. Robertson, *Predictors of COVID-19-Confirmed Cases and Fatalities in 883 US Counties with a Population of 50,000 or More: Estimated Effect of Initial Prevention Policies*, 98 J. URB. HEALTH 205, 206, 208–09 & tbl. 1 (2021) (finding that, in the studied U.S. counties, the incidence of COVID-19 infections and deaths, holding constant county population size, went up as population density increased); Mohammed Sarmadi et al., *Association of COVID-19 Distribution with Air Quality, Sociodemographic Factors, and Comorbidities: An Ecological Study of US States*, 14 AIR QUALITY, ATMOSPHERE & HEALTH 455, 456, 457 tbl. 2 (2021) (finding that, ceteris paribus, state-level increases in population density raised the number of COVID-19 infections and deaths per 100,000 state residents, and also added to the rate at which fatalities occurred among state COVID-19 cases); Karla Therese L. Sy et al., *Population Density and Basic Reproductive Number of COVID-19 Across United States Counties*, 16(4) PLoS ONE art. 0249271, at 1, 5, 6 tbl. 1 (models 2 & 3) (2021) (studying counties that had more than 25 reported COVID-19 cases during the period of exponential numerical growth in cases, and thus including data for 1,151 counties out of the 3,221 counties in the United States; finding that, ceteris paribus, R_0 went up as population density increased).

[14] *E.g.*, William J. Ripple et al., *World Scientists' Warning of a Climate Emergency 2021*, 71 BIOSCIENCE 894 (2021). *See also* Max Callaghan et al., *Machine-Learning-Based Evidence and Attribution Mapping of 100,000 Climate Impact Studies*, 11 NATURE CLIMATE CHANGE 966, 968 (2021) (estimating from a set of research documents compiled by the investigators that 85 out of every 100 people globally may already have been affected by human-generated changes in climate). *Cf.* WORLD METEOROLOGICAL ORG., STATE OF THE CLIMATE 2020, at 5 (WMO-No. 1264, 2021) (summarizing recent changes in climate and phenomena related to atmospheric warming), https://public.wmo.int/en/our-mand ate/climate/wmo-statement-state-of-global-climate.

[15] AM. PUB. HEALTH ASS'N, THE LANCET COUNTDOWN ON HEALTH AND CLIMATE CHANGE: POLICY BRIEF FOR THE UNITED STATES OF AMERICA (2021); Camilo Mora et al., *Over Half of Known Human Pathogenic Diseases Can Be Aggravated by Climate Change*, 12 NATURE CLIMATE CHANGE 869, 873 fig. 4 (2022) (finding that, of 375 infectious diseases documented in *Homo sapiens*, climate-associated hazards have worsened 218, that is, 58 percent of the 375; finding, too, that such hazards have had consistently beneficial effects on just nine diseases).

[16] Intergovernmental Panel on Climate Change, *Summary for Policymakers*, *in* CLIMATE CHANGE 2021: THE PHYSICAL SCIENCE BASIS 5–6 (2021)

[hereinafter *IPCC Summary for Policymakers*], https://www.ipcc.ch/rep
ort/ar6/wg1/#FullReport.

 Accord, Shiv Priyam Raghuraman et al., *Anthropogenic Forcing and
Response Yield Observed Positive Trend in Earth's Energy Imbalance*, 12
NATURE COMM. art. 4577, at 1, 7 (2021), https://doi.org/10.1038/s41
467-021-24544-4.

[17] Sara I. Zandalinas et al., *Global Warming, Climate Change, and Environmental
Pollution: Recipe for a Multifactorial Stress Combination Disaster*, 26 TRENDS
IN PLANT SCI. 588, 589 fig. 1A, 1B (2021).

 In each decade since 1880, yearly surface (land and ocean) temperatures
on Earth have risen by an average of 0.08 degrees Centigrade, that is,
by an average of 0.14 degrees Fahrenheit, but from 1981 through 2021,
the average yearly increase was more than twice as large (0.18 degrees
Centigrade or 0.32 degrees Fahrenheit). NAT'L OCEANIC & ATMOSPHERE
ADMIN., GLOBAL CLIMATE REPORT—ANNUAL 2021 (2022), https://www.
ncdc.noaa.gov/sotc/global/202113 (last visited Aug. 11, 2022). *See also*
Panfeng Zhang et al., *Observed Changes in Extreme Temperature over the
Global Land Based on a Newly Developed Station Daily Dataset*, 32 J. CLIMATE
8489, 8506 (2021) (studying air temperatures over land during the period
from 1951 to 2015; concluding that, inter alia, average global change in
'most extreme temperature indices occurred after the mid-1970s,' with
'generally … no significant change' before then); *IPCC Summary for
Policymakers*, *supra* note 16, at 9 (concluding inter alia that surface-level
temperatures after 1970 rose globally more 'than in any other 50-year
period over at least the last 2000 years').

[18] Alessandro Dosio et al., *Extreme Heat Waves under 1.5°C and 2°C Global
Warming*, 13 ECON. RES. LETTERS art. 054006, at 1, 7–8 (2018); E. M.
Fischer et al., *Increasing Probability of Record-Shattering Climate Extremes*,
11 NATURE CLIMATE CHANGE 689, 690, 694 (2021).

[19] Data for the period from 1961 to 2019 show that the United States
experienced a steady increase in the decadal frequency, duration (in days),
and intensity of heat waves, as well as in the mean duration (in days)
of the yearly heat-wave season. U.S. Envtl. Protection Agency, Climate
Change Indicators: Heat Waves, https://www.epa.gov/climate-indicat
ors/climate-change-indicators-heat-waves (last visited July 20, 2022).

[20] Efi Rousi et al., *Accelerated Western European Heatwave Trends Linked to
More-Persistent Double Jets over Eurasia*, 13 NATURE COMM. art, 3851, at
1, 2–3 & fig. 1 (2022) (identifying trends in the incidence and intensity
of heat waves in mid-latitude areas of the northern hemisphere of the
planet during the years 1979 through 2020; labeling Europe 'a heatwave
hotspot'), https://doi.org/10.1038/s41467-022-31432-y.

[21] Guo-Yu Ren, *Urbanization as a Major Driver of Urban Climate Change*, 6
ADVANCES IN CLIMATE CHANGE RES. 1 (2015) (observing that, compared

to suburban and rural areas, cities typically have 'higher surface air temperature, weaker mean wind speed, and lower relative humidity'). Also see Lidia Lazarova Vitanova, *How Urban Growth Changes the Heat Island Effect and Human Thermal Sensations over the last 100 Years and Towards the Future in a European City?*, 28 Meteorological Applications art. e2019, at 1, 2, 5–6. 9 (2021) (studying Sofia, Bulgaria; observing that, between the years 1878 and 2012, the residential section of Sofia underwent 'a significant increase … due to increased population and urbanization'; finding that the temperature of the air in the central portion of Sofia at 0600 local time was about 4.0 degrees Centigrade hotter in 2012 than in 1878), https://rmets.onlinelibrary.wiley.com/doi/epdf/10.1002/met.2019. A difference of 4 degrees Centigrade is equivalent to a difference of 7.2 degrees Fahrenheit.

[22] Cascade Tuholske et al., *Global Urban Population Exposure to Extreme Heat*, 118(41) Proc. Nat'l Acad. Sci. art. e2024792118, at 1, 2, 3 (2021) (concluding that very hot air temperatures were experienced in 2016 by 1.7 billion people globally, or almost one-fourth of the world population; finding that urban-population growth was responsible for two-thirds, and the heat-island tendency of urban areas was responsible for one-third, of the greater exposure to extreme heat worldwide between 1983 and 2016, with exposure measured in billions of person-days annually); Cascade Tuholske et al., *Supplementary Information for Global Urban Population Exposure to Extreme Heat* 15 tbl. S2 (2021), https://www.pnas.org/content/suppl/2021/09/28/2024792118.DCSupplemental. Substantial urbanization has occurred across the world since the middle of the twentieth century: The share of the world population that resided in an urban area nearly doubled from 30 percent in 1950 to 55 percent in 2018. U.N. Dep't of Econ. & Soc. Affairs, Population Div., World Urbanization Prospects: The 2018 Revision 9 (2019). The criteria for an area to be classified as 'urban' are established by each nation. *Id.* at 10 box I.1.

[23] Long Cao et al., *Importance of Carbon Dioxide Physiological Forcing to Future Climate Change*, 107(21) Proc. Nat'l Acad. Sci. 9513 (2010). Carbon dioxide is not the only gas that has caused climate warming. Other gases (for example, methane) have also warmed the climate, and although these gases have added less to climate warming than carbon dioxide, their ability to keep heat in the atmosphere is greater than that of carbon dioxide. U.S. Envtl. Protection Agency, Summary Report: Global Anthropogenic Non-CO_2 Greenhouse Gas Emissions: 1990–2030, at 2–3 (2012). The gases collectively have been making a steadily greater contribution to warming the atmosphere. World Meteorological Org. & Global Atmosphere Watch, WMO Greenhouse Gas Bull. No. 17, at 3 fig. 3 (2021).

[24] Susan Solomon et al., *Irreversible Climate Change Due to Carbon Dioxide Emissions*, 106(6) PROC. NAT'L ACAD. SCI. 1704 (2009); Katarzyna B. Tokarska & Kirsten Zickfeld, *The Effectiveness of Net Negative Carbon Dioxide Emissions in Reversing Anthropogenic Climate Change*, 10 ENVTL. RES. LETTERS art. 094013 (2015).

[25] Samuel Asumadu Sarkodie et al., *Global Effect of Urban Sprawl, Industrialization, Trade and Economic Development on Carbon Dioxide Emissions*, 15 ENVTL. RES. LETTERS art. 034049, at 1, 4, 6 tbl. 1 (regression models 1, 5, and 10) (2020).

[26] Rui Li et al., *The CO_2 Emissions Drivers of Post-Communist Economies in Eastern Europe and Central Asia*, 11(9) ATMOSPHERE art. 1019, at 1, 5, 7–8 tbl. 2, 10 (2020) (regression model 1, which held constant, inter alia, national energy consumption per person and national gross domestic product per ton of oil used), https://doi.org/10.3390/atmos11091006.

[27] Chulin Pan et al., *How Do the Population Structure Changes of China Affect Carbon Emissions? An Empirical Study Based on Ridge Regression Analysis*, 13(6) SUSTAINABILITY, art. 3319, at 1, 5, 6, 11–12 & tbl. 8 (2021) (holding constant (1) the share of the total population that was of working age. that is, 15–64, (2) the share of the employed population that was engaged in manufacturing, and (3) the level of economic development).

[28] Jared B. Fitzgerald et al., *Working Hours and Carbon Dioxide Emissions in the United States, 2007–2013*, 96 SOC. FORCES 1851, 1858–60, 1866 tbl. 4 (2018) (holding constant, inter alia, gross domestic product per person, mean household size, and percentage of the population that was employed).

[29] INTERGOVERNMENTAL PANEL ON CLIMATE CHANGE, CLIMATE CHANGE 2022: MITIGATION OF CLIMATE CHANGE. SUMMARY FOR POLICYMAKERS, at [41] C.7.1 (Working Group III Contribution to the Sixth Assessment Report) ([2022]).

[30] Tim Dyson, *The Role of the Demographic Transition in the Process of Urbanization*, 37(Supp.) POPULATION & DEV. REV. 34, 38, 47, 48 (2011).

[31] *Supra* note 21.

[32] Lahouari Bounoua et al., *Impact of Urbanization on US Surface Climate*, 10 ENVTL. RES. LETTERS art. 084010, at 1, 8 (2015) (study of the continental United States). The authors report the differences that they find in degrees Centigrade.

[33] Daniel Meierrieks, *Weather Shocks, Climate Change and Human Health*, 138 WORLD DEV. art. 105228, at 1, 4 & n.6, 6, 9, 11 (2021) (analyzing data on 170 nations for the period 1960–2016). *See also* A. M. Vicedo-Cabrera et al., *The Burden of Heat-Related Mortality Attributable to Recent Human-Induced Climate Change*, 11 NATURE CLIMATE CHANGE 492 (2021) (analyzing data covering 732 places in a total of 43 nations worldwide during the years 1991–2018; finding that, in the warmest four successive

months of these years, an average of about 0.6 percent of all deaths, and 37.0 percent of heat-linked deaths, were due to climate warming caused by humans).

[34] U.N. ENVIRONMENT PROGRAMME, SPREADING LIKE WILDFIRE: THE RISING THREAT OF EXTRAORDINARY LANDSCAPE FIRES 6, 10, 34, 36 (2022). Wildfires, in turn, further climate change by adding large amounts of greenhouse gases to the atmosphere. *Id.* at 6, 10, 35.

[35] Colin S. Gannon & Nik C. Steinberg, *A Global Assessment of Wildfire Potential under Climate Change Utilizing Keetch-Byram Drought Index and Land Cover Classifications*, 3 ENVTL. RES. COMM. art. 035002, at 1, 2, 4, 9–10 (2021). *See also* Adam J. P. Smith et al., *Climate Change Increases the Risk of Wildfires*, SCIENCEBRIEF REV., at 1 (Sept. 2020) (concluding from recently published research that climate warming is increasing the incidence as well as the intensity of wildfires 'in many regions around the world').

[36] Gongbo Chen et al., *Mortality Risk Attributable to Wildfire-Related $PM_{2.5}$ Pollution: A Global Time Series Study in 749 Locations*, 5 LANCET PLANET HEALTH e-579 (2021) (analyzing data on daily counts of deaths in cities located in no fewer than 28 nations during the period 2000–2016; finding that a rise in the three-day moving-average of exposure to fine particulate matter from wildfires increased the relative risk of death from all causes, from respiratory disease, and from cardiovascular disease).

[37] Andrea Duane et al., *Towards a Comprehensive Look at Global Drivers of Novel Extreme Wildfire Events*, 165 CLIMATIC CHANGE art. 43, at 1, 2 (2021).

[38] Gannon & Steinberg, *supra* note 35, at 1, 4, 6 fig. 2(c) & 2(d), 7 fig. 3(c) & 3(d). The number of houses in areas of urban-wildland contact has been growing by approximately 350,000 annually in the United States. Marshall Burke et al., *The Changing Risk and Burden of Wildfire in the United States*, 118(2) PROC. NAT'L ACAD. SCI. art. e2011048118, at 1, 1, 2 fig. 1(C) (2021). This growth raises the risk of wildfires in the United States as well as the number of Americans who are exposed to wildfires. DEMOGRAPHY AND THE ANTHROPOCENE, *supra* note 1, at 22–23.

[39] Teresa Armada Brás et al., *Severity of Drought and Heatwave Crop Losses Tripled Over the Last Five Decades in Europe*, 16 ENVTL. RES. LETTERS art. 065012, at 1, 2, 4, 8, 10–12 (2021).

[40] Mengistu M. Maja & Samuel F. Ayano, *The Impact of Population Growth on Natural Resources and Farmers' Capacity to Adapt to Climate Change in Low-Income Countries*, 5 EARTH SYSTEMS & ENV'T 271, 279 (2021) (reviewing research; concluding that human-population growth has had a range of negative effects on the biosphere and agriculture in developing nations).

[41] Roshen Fernando et al., *Global Economic Impacts of Climate Shocks, Climate Policy and Changes in Climate Risk Assessment* 21 tbl. 7 (Climate & Energy

Econ. Discussion Paper, Brookings Inst., 2021) (providing estimates of the impact of severe weather events on the production of eight categories of crops in 224 nations during the period 1961–2018); Steve Miller et al., *Heat Waves, Climate Change, and Economic Output*, 19 J. Eur. Econ. Ass'n, 1, 14, 34 (2021) (studying heat waves on the planet during 1979–2016). In addition, see Demography and the Anthropocene, *supra* note 1, at 27–28.

[42] Ariel Ortiz-Bobea et al., *The Historical Impact of Anthropogenic Climate Change on Global Agricultural Productivity*, 11 Nature Climate Change 306 (2021) (using data on 172 nations; estimating that, from the early 1960s to 2015, human-caused changes in the climate have probably curtailed global agricultural productivity by fully one-fifth), https://doi.org/10.1038/s41558-021-01000-1.

[43] Maximilian Kotz et al., *Day-to-Day Temperature Variability Reduces Economic Growth*, 11 Nature Climate Change 319 (2021) (studying variations in air temperature across regions of the world during the period 1979–2018; finding that regional economic growth decreased by at least five percent for each 1° C increase in air-temperature variability). *Accord*, Matthew E. Kahn et al., *Long-Term Macroeconomic Effects of Climate Change: A Cross-Country Analysis* 7, 47 (Int'l Monetary Fund, Working Paper No. 19/215, 2019) (studying 174 nations during the period 1960–2014; finding that yearly air-temperature deviations of 0.01° C from the historical norm reduced the growth of income by 0.0543 percentage points annually).

[44] Fischer et al., *supra* note 18.

[45] Fernando et al., *supra* note 41, at 23–24 tbls. 9–12. Annual data on 80 developing nations and 27 developed nations for the years 1961–2014 indicate that 'temperature shocks' from climate change were responsible for at least brief increases in the consumer price index. K. Mukherjee & B. Quattara, *Climate and Monetary Policy: Do Temperature Shocks Lead to Inflationary Pressures?*, 167 Climatic Change art. 32, at 1, 3, 5, 14 (2021). The economic consequences of future climate change, therefore, will plausibly include instances of inflation, though not necessarily long-lasting inflation, in the cost of products and services.

[46] M. James Salinger, *Climate Variability and Change: Past, Present and Future—An Overview*, 70 Climatic Change 9, 23 tbl. 1, 27 (2005).

[47] During the half-century from 1970 through 2019, the worldwide economic cost of disasters involving droughts, extreme temperatures, floods, landslides, storms, and wildfires increased each decade—from $175.4 billion in 1970–1979 to $1,381 billion ($1.381 trillion) in 2010–2019. Global costs were thus roughly 7.9 times higher in 2010–2019 than in 1970–1979. World Meteorological Org., WMO Atlas of Mortality and Economic Losses from Weather, Climate and Water Extremes (1970–2019), at 19 fig. 4 (2021) (costs in nominal U.S. dollars).

Out of the total \$3.6 trillion in these costs during 1970–2019, almost two-fifths were incurred during 2010–2019. Calculated from *id*. at 19 fig. 4 ($1.381 \div 3.6 = 0.384 \times 100 = 38.4\%$). Human mortality attributable to weather- and climate-linked disasters, however, was much lower in 2010–2019 than in prior decades because of improvements in early-warning systems. *Id*. at 16, 19 fig. 4. See *id*. at 12 for the definition of a 'disaster.'

[48] Nat'l Ocean Serv., *What is the Difference Between a Hurricane and a Typhoon?* https://oceanservice.noaa.gov/facts/cyclone.html.

[49] Thomas Knutson et al., *Tropical Cyclones and Climate Change Assessment—Part II: Projected Response to Anthropogenic Warming*, 101 BULL. AM. METEOROLOGICAL SOC'Y E303, E317–E318 (2020), https://doi.org/10.1175/BAMS-D-18-0194.1. A change of two degrees Celsius is equivalent to a change of 3.6 degrees Fahrenheit.

See also Thomas R. Knutson et al., *Climate Change is Probably Increasing the Intensity of Tropical Cyclones*, SCIENCEBRIEF REV., at 1, 3 (March 2021) (finding that, in the majority of climate-modelling studies, climate warming is not expected to raise the annual frequency of tropical cyclones, but that climate warming is expected 'to increase substantially' the proportion of all cyclones that are in category 4 and category 5; and noting that, among the cyclones observed to date, uncertainty exists as to whether the increased intensities of cyclones have been due to human-caused climate warming or are the result of natural variation), https://doi.org/10.5281/zenodo.4570334. *Cf.* Savin S. Chand et al., *Declining Tropical Cyclone Frequency under Global Warming*, NATURE CLIMATE CHANGE, June 27, 2022, at 1 (using two datasets to estimate the global incidence of tropical cyclones from the middle of the nineteenth century to the year 2010; finding that, for the world as a whole, a long-term secular decline has occurred in the average yearly number of tropical cyclones), https://www.nature.com/articles/s41558-022-01388-4.

[50] Christopher R. Schwalm et al., *RCP8.5 Tracks Cumulative CO_2 Emissions*, 117(33) PROC. NAT'L ACAD. SCI. 19656, 19657 (2020) (finding that the RCP8.5 climate scenario provides 'the best match' in a model of carbon-dioxide emissions to the year 2050; noting that the RCP8.5 scenario, when extended to the year 2100, remains plausible and could cause warming by 2100 of between 3.3 and 5.4 degrees Celsius, that is, between 5.9 and 9.7 degrees Fahrenheit).

[51] Reza Marsooli et al., *Climate Change Exacerbates Hurricane Flood Hazards along US Atlantic and Gulf Coasts in Spatially Varying Patterns*, 10 NATURE COMM. art. 3785, at 1, 2, 5 (2019), https://www.nature.com/articles/s41467-019-11755-z.

[52] Paul A. O'Gorman, *Precipitation Extremes under Climate Change*, 1 CURRENT CLIMATE CHANGE REP. 49, 56 (2015). *Accord*, Stephen

Blenkinsop et al., *Climate Change Increases Extreme Rainfall and the Chance of Floods*, SCIENCEBRIEF REV., at 1 (June 2021) (observing that meteorological modelling indicates that, in 'much of the world,' climate change will be accompanied by extremes of rainfall with the possibility of attendant flooding).

See also Xingying Huang & Daniel L. Swain, *Climate Change is Increasing the Risk of a California Megaflood*, 8(32) SCI. ADV. art. eabq0995, at 1, 8 (2022) (simulating the occurrence of megafloods in the state of California; defining 'megafloods' as 'historically rare to unprecedented 30-day precipitation accumulations'; concluding that, in California, climate change 'is robustly increasing both the frequency and magnitude of extremely severe storm sequences capable of causing megaflood events'), https://www.science.org/doi/10.1126/sciadv.abq0995. California, although a single state within the United States, is globally significant: If California had been a nation in 2019, its gross domestic product would have been the fifth-largest in the world. Mark J. Perry, Am. Enterprise Inst., Putting America's Enormous $21.5T Economy into Perspective by Comparing US State GDPs to Entire Countries (2020), https://www.aei.org/carpe-diem/putting-americas-huge-21-5t-economy-into-pers pective-by-comparing-us-state-gdps-to-entire-countries.

[53] FRANK KREIENKAMP ET AL., WORLD WEATHER ATTRIBUTION, RAPID ATTRIBUTION OF HEAVY RAINFALL EVENTS LEADING TO THE SEVERE FLOODING IN WESTERN EUROPE DURING JULY 2021 (2021), https://www.worldweatherattribution.org/heavy-rainfall-which-led-to-severe-flood ing-in-western-europe-made-more-likely-by-climate-change.

[54] D. L. Swain et al., *Increased Flood Exposure Due to Climate Change and Population Growth in the United States*, 8(11) EARTH'S FUTURE e2020EF001778, at 1, 2, 14–15 (2020), https://agupubs.onlinelibrary. wiley.com/toc/23284277/2020/8/11.

[55] Zandalinas et al., *supra* note 17, at 589 fig. 1B.

[56] Oleg Smirnov et al., *The Relative Importance of Climate Change and Population Growth for Exposure to Future Extreme Droughts*, 138 CLIMATIC CHANGE 41, 42–43, 51 (2016). *See also* Thomas C. Brown et al., *Adaptation to Future Water Shortages in the United States Caused by Population Growth and Climate Change*, 7 EARTH'S FUTURE 219, 220–21, 232 (2019) (studying water basins in the continental United States; predicting the geographic areas that will experience shortages of water; concluding that changes in climate along with growth in human-population size will probably lead, in numerous areas, to 'serious challenges' in water availability).

[57] M. Osman et al., *Cascading Drought-Heat Dynamics During the 2021 Southwest United States Heatwave*, 49 GEOPHYSICAL RES. LETTERS e2022GL099265, at 1, 6 (2022), https://doi.org/10.1029/2022G L099265.

[58] David J. Kaczan & Jennifer Orgill-Meyer, *The Impact of Climate Change on Migration: A Synthesis of Recent Empirical Insights*, 158 CLIMATIC CHANGE 281, 296 (2020) (reviewing studies of weather-induced migration in the past).

[59] *Id.*

[60] Min Chen & Ken Caldeira, *Climate Change as an Incentive for Future Human Migration*, 11 EARTH SYS. DYNAMICS 875, 880, 881 fig. 3(a) (2020) (estimating that, because of rising air temperatures and their environmental effects, 'hundreds of millions of people' may decide to migrate during 'the coming decades' and 'billions of people' may decide to migrate during the twenty-first century). *Accord*, VIVIANE CLEMENT ET AL., WORLD BANK, GROUNDSWELL PART II: ACTING ON INTERNAL CLIMATE MIGRATION, at x, xxii–xxiii, 12 (2021) (studying six geographic regions of the world; projecting that in 2050 as much as roughly 3 percent of the population in these regions may be within-nation migrants who (1) moved a distance of about fourteen kilometers or more and (2) remained at their destination a full decade; listing reasons that the projection is probably too low). The migration flow can be expected to involve chiefly low-skilled individuals. *See* Marc Helbling & Daniel Meierrieks, *How Climate Change Leads to Emigration: Conditional and Long-Run Effects*, 25 REV. DEV. ECON. 2323, 2340 (2021) (analyzing data on international migration during the period from 1980 to 2010), https://doi.org/10.1111/rode.12800.

[61] Muzafar Shah Habibullah et al., *Impact of Climate Change on Biodiversity Loss: Global Evidence*, ENVTL. SCI. & POLLUTION RES. [1], [11] (2021) (using data for 115 nations; concluding that, with other factors held constant, biodiversity has been negatively affected by variations in air temperature and in precipitation, that is, by manifestations of climate change, and that these variations have damaged biodiversity more than natural disasters), https://doi.org/10.1007/s11356-021-15702-8.

[62] H. O. PÖRTNER ET AL., INTERNATIONAL SCIENCE-POLICY PLATFORM ON BIODIVERSITY AND ECOSYSTEM SERVICES & INTERGOVERNMENTAL PANEL ON CLIMATE CHANGE, BIODIVERSITY AND CLIMATE CHANGE: WORKSHOP REPORT 15 (2021) (pointing out that atmospheric warming and biodiversity loss are 'mutually reinforcing ... and share common drivers through human activities'). *See also* P. DASGUPTA, THE ECONOMICS OF BIODIVERSITY: THE DASGUPTA REVIEW 131 (2021) (observing that climate change could surpass shifts in land use as the principal reason for biodiversity decline in the future and that '[b]iodiversity loss will in turn have huge implications for climate change').

[63] David Fernández et al., *Are Environmental Pollution and Biodiversity Levels Associated to the Spread and Mortality of COVDI-19? A Four-Month Global Analysis*, 271 ENVTL. POLLUTION art. 116326, at 1, 3, 5, 6 tbl. 2 (2021)

(finding that, ceteris paribus, an inverse relationship existed between the degree of biodiversity and the daily number of COVID-19 cases in 160 nations during four months in the first half of 2020). The role of human-population density in the COVID-19 pandemic is discussed earlier in Chapter Two; see *supra* notes 6 to 13 and their accompanying text.

[64] Felicia Keesing & Richard S. Ostfeld, *Impacts of Biodiversity and Biodiversity Loss on Zoonotic Diseases*, 118(17) Proc. Nat'l Acad. Sci. art. e2023540118, at 1, 7 (2021).

[65] Frédéric Gosselin & Jean-Marc Callois, *On the Time Lag between Human Activity and Biodiversity in Europe at the National Scale*, 35 Anthropocene art. 100303, at 1, 2–3, 7 (2021) (using data on twenty-two European nations for the years 1900, 1950, and 2000). *See also* Marie-Claire Danner et al., Intergovernmental Science-Policy Platform on Biodiversity and Ecosystem Services, Summary for Policymakers of the Thematic Assessment of the Sustainable Use of Wild Species 3–5, 9–10, 25 (advance unedited version, 2022) (summarizing research on human-utilized, non-domesticated animal and plant species in water- and land-based ecosystems; defining a 'non-domesticated' species, that is, a 'wild species,' as a species that has not been subject to sustained human intervention designed to develop specific traits and that is able to survive apart from humans; pointing out that wild species are 'critical for people and nature' and that the sustainable use of wild species is essential to turning around 'the global trend in biodiversity decline'; concluding that the number of wild species will be reduced by increases in the number of human beings).

[66] Jenna C. Dodson et al., *Population Growth and Climate Change: Addressing the Overlooked Threat Multiplier*, 748 Sci. Total Env't art. 141346, at 1, 2 (2020).

[67] *Supra* notes 6 to 13 and their accompanying text.

[68] Francisco Estrada & Pierre Perron, *Disentangling the Trend in the Warming of Urban Areas into Global and Local Factors*, 1504 Annals N.Y. Acad. Sci. 230, 242–43 (2021), https://doi.org/10.1111/nyas.14691. *Accord*, note 21 and its accompanying text.

[69] Xingchen Lu et al., *Impacts of Urbanization and Long-Term Meteorological Variations on Global $PM_{2.5}$ and Its Associated Health Burden*, 270 Envtl. Pollution art. 116003, at 1, 4, 5 fig. 2, 6 fig. 3.

[70] David Castells-Quintana et al., *The Urbanising Force of Global Warming: The Role of Climate Change in the Spatial Distribution of Population*, 21 J. Econ. Geography 531, 538, 550 (2021) (using data covering the period from and after 1950 for a study of cities worldwide that in 1990 had a population exceeding 300,000).

three Government Efforts to Change the Frequency of Childbearing and Immigration

1   S. STANLEY YOUNG ET AL., NAT'L ASS'N OF SCHOLARS, SHIFTING SANDS: UNSOUND SCIENCE AND UNSAFE REGULATION. REPORT #1: KEEPING COUNT OF GOVERNMENT SCIENCE: P-VALUE PLOTTING, P-HACKING, AND $PM_{2.5}$ REGULATION 23 (2021).

2   J. JOSEPH SPEIDEL ET AL., MAKING THE CASE FOR U.S. INTERNATIONAL FAMILY PLANNING ASSISTANCE 1, 4 (Johns Hopkins Univ. Bloomberg School of Pub. Health, 2009). The U.S. Agency for International Development, according to its website, is the single largest bilateral provider in the world of assistance for family planning. U.S. Agency for Int'l Dev., Family Planning and Reproductive Health (2021), https://www.usaid.gov/global-health/health-areas/family-planning (last visited June 18, 2022).

3   Speidel et al., *supra* note 2, at 11.

4   John Antonakis et al., *On Making Causal Claims: A Review and Recommendations*, 21 LEADERSHIP Q. 1086, 1087, 1088 (2010) (explaining endogeneity; pointing out that when a regression model omits an independent variable that is a cause of the dependent variable, (1) the model will yield incorrect coefficients for the included independent variables and (2) each coefficient that is estimated 'simply has no meaning. The true coefficient could be higher, lower, or even of a different sign').

5   Per M. Jensen et al., *Human Total Fertility Rate Affected by Ambient Temperatures in Both the Present and Previous Generations*, 65 INT'L J. BIOMETEOROLOGY 1837 (2021) (finding that human fertility declines when maximum monthly temperatures exceed 15–20 degrees Centigrade, that is, 59–68 degrees Fahrenheit).

6   Tests of statistical significance in social science research have other limitations, too. For example, they are inappropriately applied to data that come from a nonprobability sample of a population or to data that cover the entire population. EARL BABBIE, SURVEY RESEARCH METHODS 301–02 (2d ed., 1990).

7   David W. Rasmussen et al., *Spatial Competition in Illicit Drug Markets: The Consequences of Increased Drug Law Enforcement*, 23 REV. REGIONAL STUD. 219 (1993).

8   Kim Moeller & Morten Hesse, *Drug Market Disruption and Systemic Violence: Cannabis Markets in Copenhagen*, 10 EUR. J. CRIMINOLOGY 206, 218 (2013).

9   FRANS L. LEEUW WITH HANS SCHMEETS, EMPIRICAL LEGAL RESEARCH: A GUIDANCE BOOK FOR LAWYERS, LEGISLATORS, AND REGULATORS 122–25 (2016).

[10] Citations to relevant research are in LARRY D. BARNETT, DEMOGRAPHY AND THE ANTHROPOCENE 62–64 (2021) [hereinafter DEMOGRAPHY AND THE ANTHROPOCENE].

[11] EPA's Enforcement Program: Taking the Environmental Cop Off the Beat, Hearing Before the Subcomm. on Oversight & Investigations of the House Comm. on Energy & Commerce, 116th Cong., Feb. 26, 2019 (statement of Jay P. Shimshack) (summarizing the conclusions of empirical research), https://energycommerce.house.gov/committee-activ ity/hearings/hearing-on-epas-enforcement-program-taking-the-enviro nmental-cop-off-the. Notably, the culture of a society, inter alia, affects the degree to which business entities abide by government environmental directives. Ara Jo, *Culture and Compliance: Evidence from the European Union Emissions Trading Scheme*, 64 J. L. & ECON. 181 (2021).

[12] Anne H. Gauthier, *The Impact of Family Policies on Fertility in Industrialized Countries: A Review of the Literature*, 26 POPULATION RES. & POL'Y REV. 323, 331, 334, 339 (2007). *Accord*, Jochen René Thyrian et al., *Changing Maternity Leave Policy: Short-term Effects on Fertility Rates and Demographic Variables in Germany*, 71 SOC. SCI. & MED. 672, 673, 674 (2010) (studying a region of Germany; using data on births in the region over 23 months after the adoption of new government regulations promoting maternity leave and financial support for childbearing; finding that the regulations, which took effect in January 2007, had no impact on the rate of childbearing); Asiya Validova, *Pronatalist Policies and Fertility in Russia: Estimating Tempo and Quantum Effects*, 46 COMP. POPULATION STUD. 425, 427, 446 (2021) (assessing the effect of a 'dramatic' change in policy by the government of Russia during 2007 that sought to increase the frequency with which couples produced at least two births; concluding that, despite a short-term impact, the policy in the end affected when births occurred, that is, the timing of births, and had little long-term influence on the number of births). Additional supporting research is cited in DEMOGRAPHY AND THE ANTHROPOCENE, *supra* note 10, at 63 n.51.

[13] See, for example, LARRY D. BARNETT, THE PLACE OF LAW: THE ROLE AND LIMITS OF LAW IN SOCIETY 440 n.67 (2011); ch. 1 nn.195 to 197 and accompanying text in LARRY D. BARNETT, SOCIETAL STRESS AND LAW (forthcoming 2023).

Additional evidence that government actions seeking to restrict access to abortion do not have a substantial, long-term effect on the incidence of abortion in the United States is found in the following studies:

- Nichole Austin & Sam Harper, *Quantifying the Impact of Targeted Regulation of Abortion Provider Laws on US Abortion Rates: A Multi-State Assessment*, 100 CONTRACEPTION 374, 375, 377 (2019) (concluding that during the period 1991 to 2014 the abortion rate, that is, the number of therapeutic abortions per 1,000 females 15–44 years old, was not significantly changed by (1) state law/policy that forced abortion clinics to satisfy the standards set for ambulatory surgical centers or (2) state law/policy that required persons who perform abortions to have received from a geographically close hospital the right to admit patients to the hospital).

- Susan L. Frankel, Abortion Policy Implementation: Understanding the Availability of Abortion Services in the United States 9–10, 89, 111, 137 tbl. 6.3, 143 (Dec. 1988) (unpublished Ph.D. dissertation, Univ. of New Hampshire (on file with author) (finding a statistically insignificant relationship, in both 1976 and 1982, between an index of the restrictiveness of law on abortion in each state and the state abortion rate).

- Mark Gius, *Using the Synthetic Control Method to Determine the Effect of Ultrasound Laws on State-Level Abortion Rates*, 47 ATLANTIC ECON. J. 205, 209, 211, 213 (2019) (concluding that law requiring pregnant women to view ultrasound images of their fetuses prior to terminating their pregnancies did not have a statistically significant effect on the abortion rate).

- Marshall H. Medoff, *State Abortion Policy and Unintended Birth Rates in the United States*, 129 SOC. INDICATORS RES. 589, 590–92, 593, 596 (2016) (finding that state rates of unintended births among women 15–44 years old were not significantly affected by (1) the absence of Medicaid funding for abortions, (2) state-law requirements for the involvement of parents in decisions by their minor daughters to abort a pregnancy, (3) state-law requirements that pregnant women receive counseling prior to aborting their pregnancies, and (4) state-law requirements that pregnant women, after requesting an abortion, delay undergoing the abortion for a designated number of days).

In addition, see Rosana Peiró et al., *Does the Liberalisation of Abortion Laws Increase the Number of Abortions? The Case Study of Spain*, 11 EUR. J. PUB. HEALTH 190 (2001) (finding that a relaxation of law-based restrictions on access to abortion in Spain did not alter the abortion rate among women in that country because pregnant women in Spain, before Spain eased its restrictions on abortion, terminated their pregnancies in other countries).

[14] Jeffrey Edmeades et al., *Methodological Innovation in Studying Abortion in Developing Countries: A 'Narrative' Quantitative Survey in Madhya Pradesh, India*, 4 J. MIXED METHODS RES. 176, 177 (2010) (observing that precise statistical information regarding 'the prevalence and determinants of abortion are extremely limited for most developing country settings'). *See also* Thália Barreto et al., *Investigating Induced Abortion in Developing Countries: Methods and Problems*, 23 STUD. FAM. PLAN. 159 (1992).

[15] *E.g.*, Ian Lowe et al., *Population and Climate Change* 21 (Sustainable Population Australia, Discussion Paper, 2022); Jane N. O'Sullivan, *Revisiting Demographic Transition: Correlation and Causation in the Rate*

of Development and Fertility Decline 8 (paper presented at the IUSSP International Population Conference, Aug. 26–31, 2013). See *infra* Part 3.3 for a discussion of the paper by Professor Lowe et al. and the paper by Dr. O'Sullivan.

An additional illustration of the belief that the programs have a large fertility-reducing impact is in the text accompanying *supra* notes 2 and 3.

[16] K. Brad Wray, *Discarded Theories: The Role of Changing Interests*, 196 Synthese 553 (2019); Arthur Koestler, The Ghost in the Machine 178 (1967).

[17] Albert Einstein, *Ernst Mach*, 17 Physikalische Zeitschrift 101, 102 (1916), *reprinted in* 6 The Collected Papers of Albert Einstein: The Berlin Years: Writings, 1914–1917, at 141, 142 (Alfred Engel trans., 1997). *Accord*, Stephen Jay Gould, The Panda's Thumb: More Reflections in Natural History 243 (1980) (observing that 'Orthodoxy can be as stubborn in science as in religion').

[18] Grant Miller & Kimberly Singer Babiarz, *Family Planning Program Effects* 21 (Nat'l Bureau of Econ. Research, Working Paper No. 20586, 2014).

[19] Gustavo Angeles et al., *A Meta-Analysis of the Impact of Family Planning Programs on Fertility Preferences, Contraceptive Method Choice and Fertility* 1, 13, 15–16 (Carolina Population Ctr., MEASURE *Evaluation* Working Paper No. 01–30, 2001) (studying Bolivia, China, India, Indonesia, Kenya, Morocco, Peru, Philippines, Tanzania, Tunisia, Zimbabwe).

[20] Anrudh K. Jain & John A. Ross, *Fertility Differences Among Developing Countries: Are They Still Related to Family Planning Program Efforts and Social Settings?*, 38 Int'l Persp. on Sexual & Reprod. Health 15 (2012). The Jain-Ross study quantified family-planning program strength using a four-factor index comprised of policy, services, evaluation, and access.

[21] *Id*. at 20.

[22] *Id*. at 22 app. tbl. 1.

[23] *Id*. at 20 tbl. 3 (model 1). All Variance Inflation Factor scores were less than 2.30, indicating that collinearity among the independent variables was not problematic. Cook's Distance score for one country (Jordan) exceeded the threshold $(4/n)$ above which a case is probed as a possible influential outlier in ordinary least-squares regression. *E.g.*, Tom Van der Meer et al., *Influential Cases in Multilevel Modeling: A Methodological Comment*, 75 Am. Sociol. Rev. 173, 177 (2010). However, the omission of Jordan from the data did not materially change the unstandardized and standardized regression coefficients that were estimated. Consequently, Jordan was deemed not to be an influential outlier and was retained. The data for the regression analysis thus included all forty countries.

[24] Standardized coefficients, along with unstandardized coefficients, can be estimated simultaneously in Stata® IC version 12.1 with the command REGRESS [dependent variable] [independent variables], BETA. StataCorp,

STATA REFERENCE MANUAL RELEASE 12, at 1679, 1681, 1684 (2011); UCLA STATISTICAL METHODS & DATA ANALYSIS, REGRESSION WITH STATA CHAPTER 1 – SIMPLE AND MULTIPLE REGRESSION [28–29] (2021), https://stats.oarc.ucla.edu/stata/webbooks/reg/chapter1/regressionwith-stata chapter-1-simple-and-multiple-regression.

25 Martha J. Bailey, *Reexamining the Impact of Family Planning Programs on US Fertility: Evidence from the War on Poverty and the Early Years of Title X*, 4 AM. ECON. J.: APPLIED ECON., April 2012, at 62, 87.

26 Computed from U.S. CENSUS BUREAU, STATISTICAL ABSTRACT OF THE UNITED STATES: 1981, at 58 tbl. 83 (102d ed., 1981).

27 Robert M. Marsh, *Modernization Theory, Then and Now*, 13 COMP. SOCIOL. 261, 270 (2014) (observing that the social-economic development of a society is typically associated with a decrease in fertility that is related to a shift in 'norms, values, attitudes and behavior').

28 *E.g.*, Biodiversity & Fam. Planning Task Force, Int'l Union for Conservation of Nature, WCC Resolution 072 (2020) ('removing barriers to rights-based voluntary family planning now would have significant impacts on long-term population size and therefore reduce some pressures on the environment').

29 *See* JOHN BONGAARTS ET AL., FAMILY PLANNING PROGRAMS FOR THE 21ST CENTURY: RATIONALE AND DESIGN 43 (2012) concluding that '[t]he choice of voluntary family planning programs as the principal policy instrument for reducing fertility is based largely on the ... unsatisfied demand for contraception').

30 *See* Ronald Freedman, *Do Family Planning Programs Affect Fertility Preferences? A Literature Review*, 28 STUD. FAM. PLAN. 1, 10–11 (1997) (concluding from a review of published research that the availability of family planning may not influence the number of births preferred by childbearing-age individuals but may build on large-scale social-economic change to bring out the change-induced 'latent' maximum number of births wanted by such individuals).

31 Arun S. Hendi, *Globalization and Contemporary Fertility Convergence*, 96 SOC. FORCES 215, 233–34 (2017) (concluding that societies undergo declines in childbearing as they experience (1) social-economic development and (2) interactions with other societies that reduce, in the less-developed societies, the number of children wanted and the completed size of families).

32 *See* Dominik Paprotny, *Measuring Central and Eastern Europe's Socio-Economic Development Using Time Lags*, 127 SOC. INDICATORS RES. 939 (2016) (suggesting time lags as a new measure of between-nation social-economic differences and change).

[33] U.N. DEVELOPMENT PROGRAMME, HUMAN DEVELOPMENT REPORT 104–05 (1990); Michal Litwiński, *The Evolution of Idea of Socio-Economic Development*, 16 EKONOMIA I PRAWO. ECONOMICS & L. 449, 454–56 (2017).

[34] Mahmoud Salari, *The Impact of Intergenerational Cultural Transmission on Fertility Decisions*, 58 ECON. ANALYSIS & POL'Y 88, 98 (2018).

[35] Joshua Conrad Jackson et al., *Tight Cultures and Vengeful Gods: How Culture Shapes Religious Belief*, 150 J. EXPERIMENTAL PSYCHOL.: GEN. 2057, 2074 (2021).

[36] Bojana Pinter et al., *Religion and Family Planning*, 21 EUR. J. CONTRACEPTION & REPRODUCTIVE HEALTH CARE 486 (2016).

[37] Lowe et al., *supra* note 15, at 21, 25, 43.

[38] The reference is in O'Sullivan, *supra* note 15, at 8. The referenced book is WARREN C. ROBINSON & JOHN A. ROSS (EDS.), THE GLOBAL FAMILY PLANNING REVOLUTION: THREE DECADES OF POPULATION POLICIES AND PROGRAMS (2007) [hereinafter THE GLOBAL FAMILY PLANNING REVOLUTION]. The 23 jurisdictions are Bangladesh, Chile, Colombia, Egypt, Ghana, Guatemala, Hong Kong, India, Indonesia, Iran, Jamaica, Kenya, Malaysia, Morocco, Nepal, Pakistan, Philippines, Republic of Korea, Singapore, Sri Lanka, Thailand, Tunisia, and Turkey.

[39] Warren C. Robinson & John A. Ross, *Family Planning: The Quiet Revolution*, *in* THE GLOBAL FAMILY PLANNING REVOLUTION, *supra* note 38, at 421, 436–37 & tbl. 24.3.

[40] A ratio scale quantifies a phenomenon with measurement units of equal size and with an absolute zero, that is, the number zero is applied when the phenomenon does not exist. An interval scale quantifies a phenomenon with measurement units of equal size, but the number zero is either not used or, if used, is arbitrary, that is, is applied when some amount of the phenomenon exists. For a full explanation of scale types (ratio, interval, ordinal, and nominal), see Anwer Khurshid & Hardeo Sahai, *Scales of Measurements: An Introduction and a Selected Bibliography*, 27 QUALITY & QUANTITY 303 (1993).

[41] John Bongaarts et al., *The Demographic Impact of Family Planning Programs*, 21 STUD. FAM. PLAN. 299, 303 (1990) [hereinafter *Demographic Impact*].

[42] The estimated reduction in the TFR attributed to family-planning programs utilized assumptions that would have affected the estimate. *Id.* at 309. Different assumptions would have produced an estimate that deviated, and perhaps deviated considerably, from the reported estimate.

[43] Of the four factors that comprised the index, just one factor dealt with the extent to which fertility-avoiding methods (contraception, sterilization, and abortion) were available in the nations. *Id.* at 302. These methods, of course, are the heart of family planning, and the relationship between their availability and the TFR may not be the same as the relationship to the TFR of the other three factors in the index.

[44] *Id.* at 309 tbl. B1.

[45] James Jaccard & Robert Turrisi, Interaction Effects in Multiple Regression 24 (2d ed., 2003).

[46] Cindy D. Kam & Robert J. Franzese, Jr., Modeling and Interpreting Interactive Hypotheses in Regression Analysis 23 (2007) (italics in original).

[47] The foregoing findings are based on levels of statistical significance, but because the nations in the study were evidently a convenience sample rather that a random sample, the use of the tests is not justified. *Supra* note 6. The numerical values of standardized regression coefficients would have been helpful, but, unfortunately, they were not reported. *Demographic Impact, supra* note 41, at 309. The utility of standardized coefficients is illustrated by the Jain-Ross study (described in the text accompanying *supra* notes 20 to 24) and the paragraph in the text after *supra* note 24.

[48] The regression coefficient for family-planning program strength was -0.0017 and its standard error was 0.0089. *Demographic Impact, supra* note 41, at 309 tbl. B1. The division of the coefficient by its standard error yields a score of $(-0.0017 \div 0.0089) = -0.191$. However, a score of ± 1.96 is required to give the regression coefficient for family-planning program strength a two-tailed probability of appearing by chance in 5 percent of all randomly selected samples drawn from a population in which family-planning program strength is unrelated to the TFR. The absolute ratio of the score required to the score obtained is thus $1.96 \div 0.191 = 10.3$. The coefficient for family-planning program strength, in other words, would have had to be more than ten times larger than it was, assuming the same standard error, in order to reach the typically used maximum criterion for rejecting the null hypothesis, viz., a probability (significance level) of .05.

[49] Kam & Franzese, *supra* note 46, at 13.

[50] See the text accompanying *supra* notes 27 to 30 in Chapter Three, and notes 21 & 22 and their accompanying text in *infra* Chapter Four. For the principal tenets of structural-functionalism theory, see Demography and the Anthropocene, *supra* note 10, at 53–57.

[51] For studies of the impact of U.S. government policy on the scale of immigration into the United States, see Demography and the Anthropocene, *supra* note 10, at 63–64 n.52. The conclusion that government does not materially alter the frequency of immigration is also reached by Emily Ryo, *The Unintended Consequences of US Immigration Enforcement Policies*, 118(21) Proc. Nat'l Acad. Sci. art. e2103000118, at 1, 5 (2021).

[52] Daniel Hummel, *Immigrant-Friendly and Unfriendly Cities: Impacts on the Presence of a Foreign-Born Population and City Crime*, 17 Int'l Migration & Integration 1211, 1218–19, 1224 tbls. 7 & 8, 1226–27 (2016).

53 Hein de Haas et al., *International Migration: Trends, Determinants, and Policy Effects*, 45 POPULATION & DEV. REV. 885, 887–88, 914 (2019).

54 Mathias Czaika & Hein de Haas, *The Effectiveness of Immigration Policies: A Conceptual Review of Empirical Evidence* 5, 23 (Univ. of Oxford Int'l Migration Inst., Working Paper No. 33, 2011).

four The Concept of a System: Ecology, Sociology, and the Social Side Effects of Law/Policy

1 Ecology has been defined as 'the study of the relationships between living organisms, including humans, and their physical environment; it seeks to understand the vital connections between plants and animals and the world around them.' Ecological Soc'y of America, *What is Ecology?* https://www.esa.org/about/what-does-ecology-have-to-do-with-me.

2 Peter J. Richerson, *Ecology and Human Ecology: A Comparison of Theories in the Biological and Social Sciences*, 4 AM. ETHNOLOGIST 1, 2 (1977).

3 William R. Burnside et al., *Human Macroecology: Linking Pattern and Process in Big-Picture Human Ecology*, 87 BIOLOGICAL REV. 194 (2012). Professor Burnside and his coauthors propose a field of study that they name 'human macroecology' and believe that it can bridge the current divide between the natural sciences and social sciences. The field of human macroecology, as they define it, would focus on interactions between humans and their environment 'across spatial and temporal scales, linking small-scale interactions with large-scale, emergent patterns and their underlying processes.' *Id.* at 195, 206.

4 Paul Shepard, *Whatever Happened to Human Ecology?* 17 BIOSCIENCE 891 (1967).

Within sociology, the subdiscipline of environmental sociology emerged during the early 1970s. Jean-Guy Vaillancourt, *Sociology of the Environment: From Human Ecology to Ecosociology*, in ENVIRONMENTAL SOCIOLOGY: THEORY AND PRACTICE 3, 5 (Michael D. Mehta & Eric Quellet eds., 1995). However, environmental sociology attracted few sociologists and largely accepted established sociological thinking rather than developing novel ideas. Donna E. Hughes, *Environmental Sociology: A Distinct Field of Inquiry?*, in ENVIRONMENTAL SOCIOLOGY: THEORY AND PRACTICE, *supra* at 61, 76–77.

5 See Richerson, *supra* note 2, at 1 (citing a book published in 1938 and authored by an ecologist; describing the ecologist as being 'interested in human ecology'); Amos Hawley, *Ecology and Human Ecology*, 22 SOC. FORCES 398 (1944) (contending that human ecology arose as a field of specialization in sociology 'in the early 1920s').

6 Rudolf Stichweh, *The Sociology of Scientific Disciplines: On the Genesis and Stability of the Disciplinary Structure of Modern Science*, 5 SCI. IN CONTEXT 3, 5 (1992).

[7] *See* Andrew K. Jorgenson et al., *Social Science Perspectives on Drivers and Responses to Global Climate Change*, 10(1) WIREs CLIMATE CHANGE art. e554, at 1 (2019) (reviewing research in anthropology, archaeology, geography, and sociology on (1) human sources of and adjustments to climate change and (2) human actions to reduce climate change).

[8] Jordan F. Besek & Richard York, *Toward a Sociology of Biodiversity Loss*, 6 SOC. CURRENTS 239 (2019).

[9] Stichweh, *supra* note 6, at 4.

[10] Mario Coccia, *The Evolution of Scientific Disciplines in Applied Sciences: Dynamics and Empirical Properties of Experimental Physics*, 124 SCIENTOMETRICS 451 (2020).

[11] *Id.* at 480.

[12] Robert Maynard Hutchins, Education and the National Purpose (lecture at Rice Univ., Feb. 13, 1962), *in* 49 RICE U. STUD., Summer 1963, at 1, 13, https://scholarship.rice.edu/handle/1911/62860.

[13] Sophie Peter, *Integrating Key Insights of Sociological Risk Theory into the Ecosystem Services Framework*, 12(16) SUSTAINABILITY art. 6437, at 1, 12–15 (2020).

[14] Alexander Backlund, *The Definition of System*, 29 KYBERNETES 444 (2000).

[15] An ecosystem is defined as 'a dynamic complex of plant, animal, and microorganism communities and the nonliving environment, interacting as a functional unit. Humans are an integral part of ecosystems.' U.N. ENVIRONMENT PROGRAMME, MILLENNIUM ECOSYSTEM ASSESSMENT, ECOSYSTEMS AND HUMAN WELL-BEING: A FRAMEWORK FOR ASSESSMENT 49 (2003) [hereinafter MILLENNIUM ECOSYSTEM ASSESSMENT].

[16] John Urry, *Sociology and Climate Change*, 57(supp. 2) SOCIOL. REV. 84, 84–85 (2009).

[17] Marion Glaser et al., *New Approaches to the Analysis of Human–Nature Relations*, *in* HUMAN–NATURE INTERACTIONS IN THE ANTHROPOCENE: POTENTIALS OF SOCIAL-ECOLOGICAL ANALYSIS 3, 4 (Marion Glaser et al. eds., 2012) (proposing the concept of 'social-ecological system' and defining such a system as 'a complex, adaptive system consisting of a bio-geophysical unit and its associated social actors and institutions').

[18] 'Societal-biosphere system' may be preferable to 'social-ecological system' in capturing the essence of the concept that offers a bridge between sociology and ecology. The word 'social' can apply to species other than *Homo sapiens*: The discipline of zoology includes ethology, the study of social aspects of nonhuman animals. EnvironmentalScience.org, *Zoology: Exploring the Animal Kingdom as Academic Pursuit* (2021), https://www.environmentalscience.org/zoology. The label 'social-ecological system' is thus potentially problematic. If the word 'social' is to be confined to *Homo sapiens*, it must refer explicitly to human beings

or be used in a context that refers only to human beings, but given the vagueness common in interpersonal discourse, such a reference may be absent.

The word 'societal' in 'societal-biosphere system' refers to organized groups of *Homo sapiens*, the species that includes present-day human beings and is the sole species in the taxonomic group *Homo* that has not become extinct. Britannica, *Homo sapiens*, https://www.britannica.com/topic/Homo-sapiens. See note 2 in *supra* Chapter Two for a definition of the word 'biosphere.'

[19] LARRY D. BARNETT, DEMOGRAPHY AND THE ANTHROPOCENE 19–31 (2021) [hereinafter DEMOGRAPHY AND THE ANTHROPOCENE]; *supra* Chapter Two.

[20] MILLENNIUM ECOSYSTEM ASSESSMENT, *supra* note 15, at 17, 86, 105. Citations to additional sources are in DEMOGRAPHY AND THE ANTHROPOCENE, *supra* note 19, at 23, 30–31.

[21] David Lockwood, *Social Integration and System Integration, in* EXPLORATIONS IN SOCIAL CHANGE 244 (George K. Zollschan & Walter Hirsch eds., 1964). The posited predisposition of a human society toward integration is a proposition of structural-functionalism theory. Moshe Hirsch & Andrew Lang, *Introduction, in* RESEARCH HANDBOOK ON THE SOCIOLOGY OF INTERNATIONAL LAW 1, 2–3 (Moshe Hirsch & Andrew Lang eds., 2018). Structural-functionalism theory as it applies to marriage and childbearing is discussed in DEMOGRAPHY AND THE ANTHROPOCENE, *supra* note 19, at 53–57.

[22] The sociological concept of integration refers to the amount of friction within a society and includes social integration as well as system integration. Social integration is concerned with the amount of friction in the relationships that exist between people while system integration is concerned with the amount of friction in the relationships that exist between societal components, that is, institutions. Lockwood, *supra* note 21, at 245.

[23] Antal Orkény & Mária Székelyi, *The Role of Trust in the Social Integration of Immigrants*, 52 DEMOGRÁFIA 124, 126–27, 146 (English ed.) (2009).

[24] Timothy M. Lenton et al., *Resilience of Countries to COVID-19 Correlated with Trust*, 12 SCI. REP. art. 75, at 1, 2–3, 9, 11–12 (2022) (using multiple linear regression to analyze the impact of trust in 72 nations); Atte Oksanen et al., *Regulation and Trust: 3-Month Follow-Up Study on COVID-19 Mortality in 25 European Countries*, 6 JMIR PUB. HEALTH SURVEILLANCE art. e19218, at 1, 2–3, 7 tbl. 3 (model 3), 9 (2020). *See also* Bishoy Louis Zaki et al., *In Trust We Trust: The Impact of Trust in Government on Excess Mortality during the COVID-19 Pandemic*, 37 PUB. POL'Y & ADMIN. 226, 232–33, 238 tbl. 4, 241 (2022) (studying residents of 27 nations in continental Europe; finding an inverse association between

degree of trust in government and within-nation temporal differences in rates of death attributable to COVID-19).

[25] Anne D. Guerry et al., *Natural Capital and Ecosystem Services Informing Decisions: From Promise to Practice*, 112(24) PROC. NAT'L ACAD. SCI. 7348, 7349 (2015).

[26] LARRY D. BARNETT, SOCIETAL STRESS AND LAW ch. 1 (forthcoming 2023) [hereinafter SOCIETAL STRESS AND LAW].

[27] Quoted in Carl Jay Bajema, *Garrett James Hardin: Ecologist, Ethicist and Environmentalist*, 12 POPULATION & ENV'T 193, 204 (1991). *See also* Garrett Hardin, *An Ecolate View of the Human Predicament*, 7 ALTERNATIVES 242, 246 (1981) (proposing education in 'ecolacy' to foster the realization that, because human beings live in an environment of interconnected parts, human interventions in the environment usually do not have a high probability of yielding the outcomes desired).

[28] Wei Huang, *How Does the One Child Policy Impact Social and Economic Outcomes?*, IZA WORLD OF LABOR, Sept. 2017, at 1, 2–3.

Instances of human-rights abuses in China under the one-birth policy have been documented. Ying Chen, *China's One-Child Policy and Its Violations of Women's and Children's Rights* N.Y. Int'l L. Rev. 1, 57–65 (2009). Such abuses, by increasing social alienation, would have reduced social integration in Chinese society. See notes 21 & 22 and their accompanying text.

[29] Francisco Zamora López & Cristina Rodríguez Veiga, *From One Child to Two: Demographic Policies in China and their Impact on Population*, 172 REVISTA ESPAÑOLA DE INVESTIGACIONES SOCIOLÓGICAS 141, 142, 154 (2020).

[30] Huang, *supra* note 28, at 9.

[31] López & Veiga, *supra* note 29, at 144–46.

On January 1, 2016, China replaced its one-birth limit with a two-birth limit; in May 2021, the Chinese government made known that it would end the two-birth limit and substitute a three-birth limit. Library of Congress, *China: Two-Child Policy Becomes Law*, GLOBAL LEGAL MONITOR, Jan. 8, 2016, https://www.loc.gov/law/foreign-news/article/china-two-child-policy-becomes-law; Brian Y. S. Wong, *With Three-Child Policy, China Is Missing the Point*, FOREIGN POL'Y, June 2, 2021, https://foreignpolicy.com/2021/06/02/with-three-child-policy-china-is-missing-the-point. Notably, the two-birth policy limit may have resulted in just a small increase in the numerical size of the population in China. Yi Zeng & Therese Hesketh, *The Effects of China's Universal Two-Child Policy*, 388 LANCET 1930, 1933 tbl. (2016) (projecting that the two-birth policy will increase the peak population of China (in billions) by $(1.445 - 1.399) = .046 \div 1.399 = 0.033 \times 100 = 3.3$ percent). *See* Yu Qin & Fei Wang, *Too Early or Too Late: What Have We Learned from the*

30-Year Two-Child Policy Experiment in Yicheng, China?, 37 DEMOGRAPHIC RES. Art. 30, at 929, 930–32, 952 (2017) (using data on a rural county in China that, from 1985 to 2015, was subject to a policy that set a two-birth maximum per woman; concluding that the two-birth maximum did not, in either the short run or the long run, substantially change the birth rate in the county).

[32] Hongbin Li et al., *Estimating the Effect of the One-Child Policy on the Sex Ratio Imbalance in China: Identification Based on the Difference-in-Differences*, 48 DEMOGRAPHY 1535, 1554–55 (2011). Because of a long-standing cultural preference for sons, China appears to have historically had a high sex ratio. Kimberly Singer Babiarz et al., *Population Sex Imbalance in China Before the One-Child Policy*, 40 DEMOGRAPHIC RES. 319, 323–24 (2019) (review of research). The one-birth policy thus operated in a cultural context that favored male children.

  See generally Emily A. Stone, *Does Mate Scarcity Affect Marital Choice and Family Formation? The Evidence for New and Classic Formulations of Sex Ratio Theory*, 55 MARRIAGE & FAM. REV. 403, 407–13, 418 (2019) (concluding from a review of research that, ceteris paribus, a high ratio of men to women raises the rate of marriage, lowers the age at which first marriages occur, reduces the incidence of nonmarital births, and increases the marriage of women to men who are higher in socio-economic status); Elizabeth Brainerd, *The Lasting Effect of Sex Ratio Imbalance on Marriage and Family: Evidence from World War II in Russia*, 99 REV. ECON. & STAT. 229, 236, 238, 241 (2017) (finding that, in Russia after World War II, the low sex ratio caused by the war (1) reduced rates of marriage and childbearing and (2) raised the divorce rate as well as the nonmarital birth rate).

[33] Lena Edlund et al., *Sex Ratios and Crime: Evidence from China*, 95 REV. ECON. & STAT. 1520, 1525, 1533 (2013) (studying the incidence of crime in China using data on arrests; combining arrests for violent crime with arrests for property crime; aggregating male arrestees with female arrestees; and measuring the crime rate as the number of arrests per 10,000 residents). The higher crime rate in China may not have been due to the larger number of males. Indeed, an increase in the sex ratio may lower the rate of violent crime. Ryan Schacht et al., *Marriage Markets and Male Mating Effort: Violence and Crime Are Elevated Where Men are Rare*, 27 HUM. NATURE 489, 490, 497 (2016) (using data on the United States).

[34] Wei Huang & Yi Zhou, *One-Child Policy, Marriage Distortion, and Welfare Loss* 4–5, 16 & n.22, 18–19, 21, 26–28 (Inst. for the Study of Labor (IZA), Discussion Paper No. 9532, 2015).

[35] Tina Wang, *Fewer Women Doing More Crime: How Has the One-Child Policy Affected Female Crime in China?*, 61 SOCIOL. Q. 87, 94, 98–99, 101 (2020).

[36] Xueyao Ma et al., *Family-to-Family Child Migration Network of Informal Adoption in China*, 7 HUMAN. & Soc. Sci. COMM. art. 48, at 1, 2, 3, 9 (Aug. 2020), https://doi.org/10.1057/s41599-020-00542-7.

[37] Xiaojia Bao et al., *Where Have All the Children Gone? An Empirical Study of Child Abandonment and Abduction in China* 13–14, 24, 26–27, 31–32, 35 (Nat'l Bureau of Econ. Res., Working Paper No. 26492, 2020).

[38] The unexpected effects of the one-birth policy were not uniformly negative. A positive effect seems to have been an increase in years of education among Chinese-born youth. Laura M. Argys & Susan L. Averett, *The Effect of Family Size on Education: New Evidence from China's One-Child Policy*, 85 J. DEMOGRAPHIC ECON. 21, 25–26, 40–41 (2019). *Accord*, Mark R. Rosenzweig & Jensen Zhang, *Do Population Control Policies Induce More Human Capital Investment? Twins, Birth Weight and China's 'One-Child' Policy*, 76 REV. ECON. STUD. 1149, 1157–58, 1172–73 (2009) (using data from sample surveys of households located in one district of a province in China; estimating that the one-birth policy increased years of schooling and rates of college enrollment among children; but describing the increase as 'modest at best').

[39] Pub. L. No. 89–110, 79 Stat. 437 (1965) (codified as amended at 52 U.S.C. § 10301 et seq. (2021)). The current version of the United States Code, including title 52, is accessible at https://uscode.house.gov/downl oad/download.shtml.

[40] 'No voting qualification or prerequisite to voting, or standard, practice, or procedure shall be imposed or applied by any State or political subdivision to deny or abridge the right of any citizen of the United States to vote on account of race or color.' *Id.* at § 2 (codified as amended at 52 U.S.C. § 10301(a)). In combatting race-grounded discrimination in voting, the Act primarily sought to protect Blacks. Thornburg v. Gingles, 478 U.S. 30, 44 n.9 (1986).

[41] Justin Levitt, *Section 5 as Simulacrum*, 123 YALE L.J. ONLINE 151, 151 (2013).

[42] Nat'l Archives Found., Voting Rights Act of 1965, https://www.archive sfoundation.org/documents/voting-rights-act-1965.

[43] SOCIETAL STRESS AND LAW, *supra* note 26, at ch. 1 pt. 1.6 & app. B. My analysis in the foregoing source is based on the findings of Adriane Fresh, *The Effect of the Voting Rights Act on Enfranchisement: Evidence from North Carolina*, 80 J. POL. 713 (2018).

[44] Changes in mortality rates lead to changes in fertility rates. Luis Angeles, *Demographic Transitions: Analyzing the Effects of Mortality on Fertility*, 23 J. POPULATION ECON. 99, 118 (2010). I disregard the effect of mortality on fertility since my focus is on existing levels of fertility, whatever their cause.

[45] Naomi Rao, *Three Concepts of Dignity in Constitutional Law*, 86 NOTRE DAME L. REV. 183, 186, 270 (2011) (pointing out that the idea of

dignity has become prevalent in the constitutional law of nations and has expanded its presence in public discourse on personal rights; observing that the idea of dignity embodies the social values that societies possess regarding personal rights).

[46] Ray Fair, *U.S. Infrastructure: 1929–2017*, at 26 (Cowles Found. Discussion Paper No. 2187, 2019). *Accord*, Larry D. Barnett, Explaining Law: Macrosociological Theory and Empirical Research 253–61 (2015).

[47] *See* Ju Uijong et al., *You or Me? Personality Traits Predict Sacrificial Decisions in an Accident Situation*, 25 IEEE Transactions on Visualization & Computer Graphics 1888, 1904–05 (2019) (concluding from experiments conducted by the authors and studies done by others that individuals who put themselves ahead of others tend to be impulsive and willing to act immorally).

[48] See *supra* note 21 and its accompanying text.

[49] See text accompanying notes 18 to 26 in *supra* Chapter Three.

[50] See citations to sources in Demography and the Anthropocene, *supra* note 19, at 65–66.

[51] M. Y. Berghauser Pont et al., *A Systematic Review of the Scientifically Demonstrated Effects of Densification*, 588 IOP Conf. Series: Earth & Environ. Sci. art. 052031, at 1 (2020); Philip Harrison et al., *Scholarship and Policy on Urban Densification: Perspectives from City Experiences*, 43 Int'l Dev. Plan. Rev. 151, 151 (2021).

[52] See citations to sources in Demography and the Anthropocene, *supra* note 19, at 66 & n.63.

[53] Bin Huang et al., *Exploring Carbon Neutral Potential in Urban Densification: A Precinct Perspective and Scenario Analysis*, 12(12) Sustainability art. 4814, at 1, 13 (2020).

[54] Adrienne Grêt-Regamey et al., *How Urban Densification Influences Ecosystem Services—A Comparison Between a Temperate and a Tropical City*, 15 Envtl. Res. Letters art. 075001, at 1, 8, 11 (2020). For a summary of the ways that trees benefit the biosphere, see Botanic Gardens Conservation Int'l, State of the World's Trees 6 (2021).

[55] Christine Haaland et al., *Challenges and Strategies for Urban Green-Space Planning in Cities Undergoing Densification: A Review*, 14 Urban Forestry & Urban Greening 760 (2015). *Accord*, Brenda Lin et al., *Understanding the Potential Loss and Inequities of Green Space Distribution with Urban Densification*, 14 Urban Forestry & Urban Greening 952, 955, 957 (2015).

[56] Text accompanying notes 6 to 13 in *supra* Chapter Two.

[57] In the United States, the COVID-19 pandemic lowered, at least temporarily, the demand for housing located in areas of high population density. Sitian Liu & Yichen Su, *The Impact of the COVID-19 Pandemic*

on the Demand for Density: Evidence from the U.S. Housing Market 1, 1–3 (Federal Res. Board of Dallas Working Paper No. 2024, 2020). https://papers.ssrn.com/sol3/papers.cfm?abstract_id=3676669.

58 Christos S. Savva, *Factors Affecting Housing Prices: International Evidence*, 12 Cyprus Econ. Pol'y Rev. 87, 90, 92, 94 tbl. 1 (2018) (using data on 24 nations in Europe).

59 Kristine Gevorgyan, *Do Demographic Changes Affect House Prices?*, 85 J. Demographic Econ. 305, 306, 313–14, 315, 317 tbl. 2 (2019) (using data on nations that are members of the Organization for Economic Co-operation and Development; estimating that a 1 percent increase in the rate of population growth caused housing prices to go up by 1.47 to 3.21 percent). *Accord*, G. Donald Jud & Daniel T. Winkler, *The Dynamics of Metropolitan Housing Prices*, 23 J. Real Estate Res. 29, 31, 33, 34 (2002) (using data on 130 metropolitan areas in the United States; estimating that a 1 percent increase in the population-growth rate produced a 1.09 percent increase in housing real prices); Shihong Zeng et al., *Population Aging, Household Savings and Asset Prices: A Study Based on Urban Commercial Housing Prices*, 11(11) Sustainability art. 3194, at 5, 8 (2019) (using data on 257 prefecture-level cities in China).

five Fertility Rates, Mean Age of Childbearing, and Childlessness

1 See Part 1.3.2 in *supra* Chapter One.

2 See note 36 in *supra* Chapter One for the source of the data in Table 5.1.

3 The data for Figure 5.1 are from U.N. Population Div., Dep't of Econ. & Soc. Affairs, *World Population Prospects 2019. File FERT/7: Age-Specific Fertility Rates by Region, Subregion and Country, 1950–2100 (Births per 1,000 Women) – Estimates, 1950–2020*, https://population.un.org/wpp/Download/Standard/Fertility (in columns 'Sub Group' and 'Files,' select respectively 'Age Composition' and 'Age-specific Fertility Rates').

4 Elizabeth Wilkins, *Low Fertility: A Review of Determinants* 11 (U.N. Population Fund, Working Paper No. 2, 2019) ('There is almost universal agreement among demographers that the postponement of childbearing has, without exception, played a key role in the decline of fertility to low levels').

5 Grazyna Jasienska, *Costs of Reproduction and Ageing in the Human Female*, 375 Phil. Transactions B Royal Soc'y art. 20190615, at 7 (2020) (observing that multiple pregnancies separated by short intervals have been found by 'many studies' to raise the probability that females who have had such pregnancies will experience age-linked illnesses), https://doi.org/10.1098/rstb.2019.0615.

[6] John Mirowsky, *Age at First Birth, Health, and Mortality*, 46 J. HEALTH & SOC. BEHAV. 32, 42 fig. 3 (2005) (analyzing data from a national sample of women in the United States).

[7] Simerpal K. Gill et al., *Association between Maternal Age and Birth Defects of Unknown Etiology—United States, 1997–2007*, at 1 (Nat'l Libr. Med. PMID 22821755, 2015), https://pubmed.ncbi.nlm.nih.gov/22821755.

[8] The data in Figure 5.2 are from U.N. Population Div., Dep't of Econ. & Soc. Affairs, *World Population Prospects 2019. File FERT/8: Female Mean Age of Childbearing by Region, Subregion and Country, 1950–2100 (Years)—Estimates, 1950–2020* [hereinafter *File FERT/8*], https://pop ulation.un.org/wpp/Download/Standard/Fertility (in columns 'Sub Group' and 'Files,' select respectively 'Age Composition' and 'Mean Age of Childbearing') (last visited Dec. 9, 2021).

[9] The impact of fertility on population growth should be studied, as it is here, using period data, not cohort data. Robert Schoen & Stefan Hrafn Jonsson, *A Diminishing Population Whose Every Cohort More than Replaces Itself*, 9 DEMOGRAPHIC RES. 111 (2003).

[10] The income level of a nation is determined by the World Bank using data on the gross national income per person in the nation; the gross national income of a nation is translated into U.S. dollars from the local currency of the nation. World Bank, Data: How Does the World Bank Classify Countries?, https://datahelpdesk.worldbank.org/knowledgeb ase/articles/378834-how-does-the-world-bank-classify-countries (last visited Dec. 11, 2021).

[11] World Bank, World Bank Country and Lending Groups, https://datah elpdesk.worldbank.org/knowledgebase/articles/906519-world-bank-country-and-lending-groups (last visited Dec. 17, 2021).

[12] Samuel Asumadu Sarkodie, *Environmental Performance, Biocapacity, Carbon & Ecological Footprint of Nations: Drivers, Trends and Mitigation Options*, 751 SCI. TOTAL ENV'T art. 141912, at 1, 2, 7 tbl. 1, 10 (models 3 through 7) (2021) (analyzing data that cover the period 1961–2016 for 188 nations and territories; concluding that jurisdiction-level economic growth, as well as increases in jurisdiction-level human-population density, are generally responsible for greater pressure on the environment; and that the environmental damage caused by economic growth is separate from the environmental damage caused by greater population density).

[13] The coefficient for the correlation between the female mean age of childbearing in middle-income nations and the female mean age of childbearing in low-income nations was r = 0.68. Also see note 35 in *supra* Chapter One.

[14] The graphs in Part 5.3 are based on data in U.N. Population Div., Dep't of Econ. & Soc. Affairs, *World Population Prospects 2019. File FERT/ 7: Age-Specific Fertility Rates by Region, Subregion and Country, 1950–2100*

(Births per 1,000 Women) – *Estimates, 1950–2020*, https://population. un.org/wpp/Download/Standard/Fertility (in columns 'Sub Group' and 'Files,' select respectively 'Age Composition' and 'Age-specific Fertility Rates') (last visited Dec. 9, 2021).

[15] For an explanation of the TFR, see Part 1.3.2 in *supra* Chapter One. For the current range of national income covered by each income category, see the text accompanying *supra* note 11 in the present chapter.

[16] Sarkodie, *supra* note 12, and accompanying text. *Cf.* LARRY D. BARNETT, DEMOGRAPHY AND THE ANTHROPOCENE 11–13 & fig. 1.3 (2021) (discussing and comparing the yearly ecological footprints from 1961 to 2016 of Africa, Asia, South America, the United States, and Western Europe).

[17] Neil Fantom & Umar Serajuddin, World Bank Group, *The World Bank's Classification of Countries by Income* 2, 3 fig. 1 (Pol'y Research Working Paper No. 7528, 2016) (count for fiscal year 1989–1990); World Bank, Data: Countries and Economies (count for fiscal year 2021–2022), https://datatopics.worldbank.org/world-development-indicators/the-world-by-income-and-region.html (follow 'Country and Indicator pages' hyperlink; on the 'Countries and Economies' page, sequentially select 'Low income' under 'Income levels' in the right column) (last visited Dec. 26, 2021).

[18] Low-income nations today are located chiefly on one continent, viz., Africa. World Bank, The World by Income, https://datatopics.worldb ank.org/world-development-indicators/the-world-by-income-and-reg ion.html.

[19] Arthur G. Bedeian & Kevin W. Mossholder, *On the Use of the Coefficient of Variation as a Measure of Diversity*, 3 ORGANIZATIONAL RES. METHODS 285, 286–87 (2000).

[20] *File FERT/8*, *supra* note 8.

[21] In middle-income nations, the female mean age of childbearing went from a low of 27.3 in 1995–2000 to 27.8 in 2015–2020, a gain of just half a year. *Id.*

[22] Tomáš Sobotka, *Childlessness in Europe: Reconstructing Long-Term Trends Among Women Born in 1900–1972*, *in* CHILDLESSNESS IN EUROPE: CONTEXTS, CAUSES, AND CONSEQUENCES 17, 19, 22 (Michaela Kreyenfeld & Dirk Konietzka eds., 2017) [hereinafter CHILDLESSNESS IN EUROPE]; Katja Köppen et al., *Childlessness in France*, in *id.*, at 77, 88.

[23] Margaret E. Greene & Ann E. Biddlecom, *Absent and Problematic Men: Demographic Accounts of Male Reproductive Roles*, 26 POPULATION & DEV. REV. 81, 81, 85 (2000). *Accord*, Michèle Tertilt et al., *Gender Gaps in Completed Fertility*, at 1, 2 (paper presented at the annual meeting of the Verein für Socialpolitik, 2015), http://hdl.handle.net/10419/113190.

[24] Roberto Matorras et al., *Decline in Human Fertility Rates with Male Age: A Consequence of a Decrease in Male Fecundity with Aging?*, 71 GYNECOLOGIC & OBSTETRIC INVESTIGATION 229 (2009).

[25] *See*, for example, Virginia Zarulli et al., *Women Live Longer than Men Even During Severe Famines and Epidemics*, 115(4) PROC. NAT'L ACAD. SCI. E832 (2018), www.pnas.org/cgi/doi/10.1073/pnas.1701535115.

[26] Renske Keizer et al., *Pathways into Childlessness: Evidence of Gendered Life Course Dynamics*, 40 J. BIOSOCIAL SCI. 863, 871 (2007). Studies, however, may not reach the same conclusion regarding the impact of a particular sociological condition. *Compare* Keizer et al. *supra with* Lynn K. White & Hyunju Kim, *The Family-Building Process: Childbearing Choice by Parity*, 49 J. MARRIAGE & FAM. 271 (1987). In this regard, the Keizer et al. study, which employed cross-sectional data on residents of The Netherlands, and the White-Kim study, which used panel data on married residents of the United States, disagree in their findings on the effect of education. Keizer et al. conclude that, ceteris paribus, the probability of childlessness among women went up with the 'highest education level' that had been 'pursued.' Keizer et al., *supra*, at 869, 872. White and Kim, on the other hand, conclude that, ceteris paribus, the likelihood of childlessness among married women declined as educational attainment rose. White & Kim, *supra*, at 273, 277 & tbl. 4 (finding that 'high education ... encourage[s] childless wives to have that first child').

[27] Maya N. Mascarenhas et al., *National Regional, and Global Trends in Infertility Prevalence Since 1990: A Systematic Analysis of 277 Health Surveys*, 9(12) PLoS MED. art. e1001356, at 3 tbl. 1, 5 (2012).

[28] Sobotka, *supra* note 22, at 26, 29 fig. 2.2, 31 fig. 2.3, 33 fig. 2.4; Tomas Frejka, *Childlessness in the United States*, in CHILDLESSNESS IN EUROPE, *supra* note 22, at 159.

[29] J. Richard Udry, *The Effect of Normative Pressures on Fertility*, 5 POPULATION & ENV'T 109, 113, 122 (1982) (studying a probability sample of Caucasian women who had been married at least once, who resided in one of 16 metropolitan areas in the United States, and who were interviewed in 1974, 1977, and 1978; measuring interviewee-anticipated reactions, by others who are closely related to the interviewee, to a pregnancy on the part of the interviewee; finding that the impact of the reactions was largest at zero parity, was progressively weaker at parities one and two, and was minimal at parities above two).

[30] See Part 3.1 in *supra* Chapter Three. The optimal research design is described in, and a study that employed it is reported in, Chester L. Britt et al., *A Reassessment of the D.C. Gun Law: Some Cautionary Notes on the Use of Interrupted Time Series Designs for Policy Impact Assessment*, 30 LAW & SOC'Y REV. 361 (1996).

[31] Paula E. Gobbi, *A Model of Voluntary Childlessness*, 26 J. POPULATION ECON. 963, 980 (2013).

[32] Caroline Sten Hartnett & Alison Gemmill, *Recent Trends in U.S. Childbearing Intentions*, 57 DEMOGRAPHY 2035, 2036–37, 2040 fig. 2 (2020) (analyzing data on intentions for future childbearing by U.S. residents aged 15–44; combining both sexes in the analysis); Sobotka, *supra* note 22, at 36, 38 (presenting percentages of women in birth cohorts in Europe who remained childless); Kryštof Zeman et al., *Cohort Fertility Decline in Low-Fertility Countries: Decomposition using Parity Progression Ratios*, 38 DEMOGRAPHIC RES. 651, 669 fig. 3 (2018) (studying cohorts of women born between 1940 and 1970 in Europe; reporting changes over time in the proportions of childless women who had first births). None of these studies was confined to women who were medically able to conceive and carry a pregnancy to term. Medical infertility is thought to be responsible for childlessness among up to one out of ten cohort members. Michaela Kreyenfeld & Dirk Konietzka, *Analyzing Childlessness*, in CHILDLESSNESS IN EUROPE, *supra* note 22, at 3, 7; text accompanying *supra* note 27.

[33] For a discussion of when population-control measures involve ethical questions, see Julia Räikkä, *Problems in Population Theory*, 31 J. SOC. PHIL. 401 (2000).

[34] Lonnie W. Aarssen & Stephanie Tzipporah Altman, *Explaining Below-Replacement Fertility and Increasing Childlessness in Wealthy Countries: Legacy Drive and the 'Transmission Competition' Hypothesis*, 4 EVOLUTIONARY PSYCHOL. 290 (2006).

[35] LARRY D. BARNETT, EXPLAINING LAW: MACROSOCIOLOGICAL THEORY AND EMPIRICAL RESEARCH ch. 1 (2015); LARRY D. BARNETT, SOCIETAL AGENTS IN LAW: A MACROSOCIOLOGICAL APPROACH 14–15 (2019) [hereinafter SAIL VOL. I].

[36] Dora L. Costa, *From Mill Town to Board Room: The Rise of Women's Paid Labor*, 14 J. ECON. PERSP. 101, 106 tbl. 1 (2000). In the United States, the labor force participation rate of married women is more significant than the labor force participation rate of unmarried women because of the prevalence of marriage among women. For example, the probability that a woman in the United States would marry by age 30 was 76 percent in 1995 and 68 percent in 2006–2010. Casey E. Copen et al., Nat'l Ctr. Health Stat., *First Marriages in the United States: Data From the 2006–2010 National Survey of Family Growth*, NAT'L HEALTH STAT. REP. 14 tbl, 3 (No. 49, 2012) (probability of first marriage). During the period from 1890 onward, more than 88 percent of all women aged 35 and older in the United States had married. Diana B. Elliott et al., *Historical Marriage Trends from 1890–2010: A Focus on Race Differences* [20] fig. 2 (SEHSD Working Paper No. 12, 2012), https://www.census.gov/library/work ing-papers/series/sehsd-wp.html.

[37] Steven Ruggles, *Marriage, Family Systems, and Economic Opportunity in the USA Since 1850, in* GENDER AND COUPLE RELATIONSHIPS 3, 16 fig. 11 (S. M. McHale et al. eds., 2016).

[38] Stanton v. Stanton, 421 U.S. 7, 14–15 (1975) (internal citation omitted).

[39] An equal protection guarantee is explicit in section 1 of the Fourteenth Amendment, which applies to state governments and their subdivisions, and implicit in the due process guarantee of the Fifth Amendment, which applies to the federal government. U.S. CONST. amends. V, XIV; Weinberger v. Wiesenfeld, 420 U.S. 636, 638 n.2 (1975).

[40] Stanton v. Stanton, 421 U.S. 7, 17 (1975).

[41] United States v. Virginia, 518 U.S. 515, 532 (1996).

[42] Sandra Day O'Connor, *Portia's Progress*, 66 N.Y.U. L. REV. 1546, 1551 (1991). *Accord*, SAIL VOL. 1, *supra* note 35, at 164–65 (mapping U.S. Supreme Court opinions since the 1870s that dealt with sex distinctions and gender roles).

[43] *See* Vinod Mishra & Russell Smyth, *Female Labor Force Participation and Total Fertility Rates in the OECD: New Evidence from Panel Cointegration and Granger Causality Testing*, 62 J. ECON. & BUS. 48, 59 tbl. 8, 60–61 (2010) (studying the relationship between the female labor force participation rate and the total fertility rate in the 28 nations that are members of the Organization for Economic Co-operation and Development; concluding that, among women, incompatibilities between the role of mother and the role of employee lower the total fertility rate in these nations, including the United States).

[44] Paula Thijs et al., *The Rise in Support for Gender Egalitarianism in the Netherlands, 1979–2006: The Roles of Educational Expansion, Secularization, and Female Labor Force Participation*, 81 SEX ROLES 594, 598–99, 601, 603 tbl. 2, 604–05 (2019) (analyzing data from fourteen nationwide sample surveys conducted from 1979 to 2006 in The Netherlands).

[45] LARRY D. BARNETT, THE PLACE OF LAW: THE ROLE AND LIMITS OF LAW IN SOCIETY 308–09, 453 n.223 (2011).

[46] *See* Stephen K. Sanderson & Joshua Dubrow, *Fertility Decline in the Modern World and in the Original Demographic Transition: Testing Three Theories with Cross-National Data*, 21 POPULATION & ENV'T 511, 518–19, 527 (2000) (finding that total fertility rates in 121 nations were reduced by, inter alia, increases in 'female empowerment,' a variable that combined the rates among females of enrollment in secondary education and participation in the labor force).

[47] Studies are inconsistent in their findings regarding the impact of education on the probability of childlessness. *Supra* note 26.

[48] Heather M. Gerling et al., *Fractured Modernization: Cultural and Structural Predictors of Attitudes on Gender Equality*, 29 INT'L REV. SOCIOL. 260, 268–69, 272 tbl. 3 (models 2 & 3) (2019).

[49] Daniel Stockemer & Aksel Sundström, *Modernization Theory: How to Measure and Operationalize it When Gauging Variation in Women's Representation?* 125 Soc. Indicators Res. 695, 696, 700, 707 tbl. 3 (2016) (analyzing data on 30 European nations inclusive of Turkey).

[50] Tomas Frejka et al., *The Two-Part Gender Revolution, Women's Second Shift and Changing Cohort Fertility*, 43 Comp. Population Studies 99, 123 (2018) (studying 11 nations in four geographic regions of the world; concluding that greater female involvement in the labor force relative to male involvement in the labor force reduced the total fertility rates of birth cohorts in these nations). *See also* Mishra & Smyth, *supra* note 43.

six Concluding Remarks

[1] Wendy K. Smith & Marianne W. Lewis, *Toward a Theory of Paradox: A Dynamic Equilibrium Model of Organizing*, 36 Acad. Mgmt. Rev. 381, 391 (2011).

[2] Robert K. Watson (quoted in Mary Skopec, *From the President's Desk*, 34(1) Okoboji Protective Ass'n Newsletter, Spring/Summer 2020, at 2).

[3] U.N. Office for Disaster Risk Reduction, Global Assessment Report on Disaster Risk Reduction 2022: Our World at Risk: Transforming Governance for a Resilient Future 17, 18 fig. 2.1 (2022). A 'disaster' is defined in *id.* at 3.

[4] Larry D. Barnett, Demography and the Anthropocene 3 n.6 (2021) [hereinafter Demography and the Anthropocene].

[5] U.N. Environment Programme, Making Peace with Nature 13, 21 (2021).

[6] E. Rignot et al., *Four Decades of Antarctica Ice Sheet Mass Balance from 1979–2017*, 116(4) Proc. Nat'l Acad. Sci. 1095 (2019).

[7] Int'l Thwaites Glacier Collaboration, Thwaites Glacier Facts, https://thwaitesglacier.org/index.php/about/facts.

[8] Erin C. Pettit et al., *Collapse of Thwaites Eastern Ice Shelf by Intersecting Fractures* (paper presented at the Fall 2021 meeting of the Am. Geophysical Union, New Orleans, Louisiana, 13–17 Dec. 2021), https://agu.confex.com/agu/fm21/meetingapp.cgi/Paper/978762. The total collapse of the Thwaites Glacier has the potential to raise sea levels around the world by an estimated 25 inches (65 centimeters). Int'l Thwaites Glacier Collaboration, Thwaites Glacier Facts, https://thwaitesglacier.org/about/facts.

[9] T. A. Scambos et al., *How Much, How Fast? A Science Review and Outlook for Research on the Instability of Antarctica's Thwaites Glacier in the 21st Century*, 153 Global & Planetary Change 16 (2017).

The Antarctic is not the only polar region that has been affected by climate change. The Arctic has been warming at least three times more rapidly than the planet as a whole. ARCTIC MONITORING & ASSESSMENT PROGRAMME, ARCTIC CLIMATE CHANGE UPDATE 2021: KEY TRENDS AND IMPACTS. SUMMARY FOR POLICYMAKERS 4 (2021); Mika Rantanen et al., *The Arctic Has Warmed Nearly Four Times Faster than the Globe Since 1979*, 3 COMM. EARTH & ENV'T art. 168, at 1, 6 (2022). The Arctic, defined as places within the Arctic Circle, encompasses, inter alia, roughly two-thirds of the island of Greenland. Rasmus Ole Rasmussen, *Greenland*, BRITANNICA ([2022]), https://www.britannica.com/place/Greenland; Editors of Encyclopaedia Britannica, *Arctic Circle*, BRITANNICA ([2022]), https://www.britannica.com/place/Arctic-Circle. Assuming no change in the average surface climate that existed during 2000–2019, ice loss in Greenland is projected to raise global sea levels about 10.8 ± 2.7 inches (274 ± 68 millimeters); the majority of this sea-level rise is expected to occur by the end of the twenty-first century. Jason E. Box et al., *Greenland Ice Sheet Climate Disequilibrium and Committed Sex-Level Rise*, 12 NATURE CLIMATE CHANGE 808, 812 (2022).

10   See Part 2.2 in *supra* Chapter Two.

11   See Part 2.1 in *supra* Chapter Two.

12   Jocelyne Piret & Guy Boivin, *Pandemics Throughout History*, 11 FRONTIERS IN MICROBIOLOGY 631 (2021).

13   Monica H. Green, *Editor's Introduction*, *in* PANDEMIC DISEASE IN THE MEDIEVAL WORLD: RETHINKING THE BLACK DEATH 9 (Monica H. Green ed., 2015). PANDEMIC DISEASE The bacterium *Yersinia pestis*, which is chiefly transmitted by fleas, is generally thought to have been responsible for the Black Death plague. Kathryn A. Glatter & Paul Finkelman, *History of the Plague: An Ancient Pandemic for the Age of COVID-19*, 134 AM. J. MED. 176, 177 (2020). The plague has not disappeared and continues to infect humans; during the period 2000–2009, the World Health Organization was informed of nearly 22,000 cases. Michelle Ziegler, *The Black Death and the Future of the Plague*, *in* PANDEMIC DISEASE, *supra*, at 259, 265–66.

14   Ricardo A. Olea & George Christakos, *Duration of Urban Mortality for the 14th Century Black Death Epidemic*, 77 HUM. BIOLOGY 291, 297 fig. 1, 300 (2005).

15   See Part 2.1 in *supra* Chapter Two.

16   John R. Stephenson, *The Problem with Dengue*, 99 TRANSACTIONS ROYAL SOC'Y OF TROPICAL MEDICINE & HYGIENE 643, 643 (2005) (observing that, during the half-century after 1950, dengue infected an estimated 50 to 100 million people worldwide and was the most common virus-caused disease among humans; attributing the increase in dengue infections during this period to, inter alia, human 'population growth').

[17] Bhavayta Mahajan, *The COVID-19 Pandemic: Why It Won't Be the Last* 3–4 (Observer Research Found., ORF Issue Brief No. 386, 2020).

[18] Andrea Swei et al., *Patterns, Drivers, and Challenges of Vector-Borne Disease Emergence*, 20 Vector-Borne and Zoonotic Diseases 159, 164, 166 (2020).

[19] Colin J. Carlson et al., *Climate Change Increases Cross-Species Viral Transmission Risk*, 607 Nature 555 (2022).

[20] See (1) Demography and the Anthropocene, *supra* note 4, at 24–25, and (2) Part 2.2 in *supra* Chapter Two.

[21] Calistus N. Ngonghala et al., *Effects of Changes in Temperature on Zika Dynamics and Control*, 18 J. Royal Soc'y Interface art. 20210165, at 9–10 (2021). *Accord*, Sadie J. Ryan et al., *Warming Temperatures Could Expose More than 1.3 Billion New People to Zika Virus Risk by 2050*, 27 Global Change Biology 84, 88–89 (2021), https://doi.org/10.1111/gcb.15384. The Zika virus, which is carried by mosquitos of the genus *Aedes*, produces severe congenital malformations in infants whose mothers are infected with the virus during pregnancy, and it raises the risk of neurological problems in adults as well as children. World Health Org., Zika Virus, https://www.who.int/news-room/fact-sheets/detail/zika-virus.

[22] Boris V. Schmid et al., *Climate-Driven Introduction of the Black Death and Successive Plague Reintroductions into Europe*, 112(10) Proc. Nat'l Acad. Sci. 3020 (2015), https://www.pnas.org/doi/full/10.1073/pnas.1412887112.

[23] While social divisions and culture receive considerable attention in the political arena and mass media, growth in the stock of knowledge does not. As a result, the public is less often aware of advances in knowledge than of societal divisions and culture. However, large increases in knowledge have occurred. Larry D. Barnett, Societal Agents in Law: A Macrosociological Approach 103–05 (2019) [hereinafter SAIL vol. 1]. For instance, the number of new chemical substances has grown by an average of more than 4 percent per year since 1800. Eugenio J. Lianos et al., *Exploration of the Chemical Space and Its Three Historical Regimes*, 116(26) Proc. Nat'l Acad. Sci. 12660, 12664 (2019).

[24] A summary of the evidence is in SAIL vol. 1, *supra* note 23, at ch. 2.

[25] See Part 3.2 and Part 3.3 in *supra* Chapter Three. Law/policy in general appears to be adopted or revised for a society-important social activity after the frequency of the activity has begun to change. Larry D. Barnett, Explaining Law: Macrosociological Theory and Empirical Evidence 47, 50–52, 56 (2015).

[26] See the text accompanying note 21 in *supra* Chapter Four.

[27] Pubin Hong et al., *Biodiversity Promotes Ecosystem Functioning Despite Environmental Change*, ECOLOGY LETTERS 1, 12 (2021), https://doi.org/10.1111/ele.13936.

[28] *See* Benjamin Faude, *International Institutions in Hard Times: How Institutional Complexity Increases Resilience*, 6 COMPLEXITY, GOVERNANCE & NETWORKS 46, 47 (2020) (contending that complexity in the world social order has generated complexity in the international arrangements created for global governance and that complexity in global-governance arrangements has had the unplanned effect of improving the resiliency of the arrangements).

[29] U.N. ENVIRONMENT PROGRAMME, GLOBAL ENVIRONMENT OUTLOOK (GEO-6): SUMMARY FOR POLICYMAKERS 4, 19 (2019).

[30] The adage is of unknown origin; it can be found in, for example, J. A. Loraine, *The Dilemma of Overpopulation*, 7 J. ROYAL C. PHYSICIANS LONDON 291, 291 (1973).

[31] Veronica Lupi & Simone Marsiglio, *Population Growth and Climate Change: A Dynamic Integrated Climate-Economy-Demography Model*, 104 ECOLOGICAL ECON. art. 107011, at 1, 8 (2021) (studying three population-control policies that differ in stringency; simulating the impact of the policies on global human welfare during the twenty-first century; concluding that population-control policies are a promising supplement to efforts designed to mitigate climate change).

[32] See the following:
- In *supra* Chapter Two, Part 2.1; notes 33, 36, & 69 and their accompanying text.
- DEMOGRAPHY AND THE ANTHROPOCENE, *supra* note 4, at 22, 26–28, 73–74.

[33] For example, higher population density raises the price of housing. Notes 58 & 59 and their accompanying text in *supra* Chapter Four. Higher housing costs will necessarily reduce the amount of living space occupied by human beings, and less space in housing lowers the fertility of childbearing-age couples. DEMOGRAPHY AND THE ANTHROPOCENE, *supra* note 4, at 65.

Childbearing is likely to be reduced by the hotter air temperatures involved in climate warming. Alan Barreca et al., *Maybe Next Month? Temperature Shocks and Dynamic Adjustments in Birth Rates*, 55 DEMOGRAPHY 1269, 1290 (2018) (studying U.S. birth rates during the period 1931–2010; concluding that hot temperatures reduced birth rates and that the reduction was from biological changes in humans, not from a lower frequency of sexual intercourse). *See also* Sarah Eissler et al., *Climatic Variability and Changing Reproductive Goals in Sub-Saharan Africa*, 57 GLOBAL ENVTL. CHANGE art. 101912, at 1, 3, 4, 9 (2019) (analyzing data from samples of women aged 15–49 in 18 nations in sub-Saharan Africa who had, within the previous ten years, married or started to cohabit;

finding that hotter air temperatures reduced the number of children that the respondents believed were ideal for them and that the respondents personally preferred).

For a discussion of heat waves, see notes 17 to 20 and their accompanying text in *supra* Chapter Two.

[34] Christopher Bystroff, *Footprints to Singularity: A Global Population Model Explains Late 20th Century Slow-Down and Predicts Peak within Ten Years*, 16(5) PLoS ONE art. e0247214, at 1, 6, 9 (2021).

Index

References to figures appear in *italic* type.